HIDDEN GIRL

HIDDEN

the true story of a modern-day child slave

GIRL

SHYIMA HALL

WITH LISA WYSOCKY

SIMON & SCHUSTER BFYR

NEW YORK   LONDON   TORONTO   SYDNEY   NEW DELHI

An imprint of Simon & Schuster Children's Publishing Division

1230 Avenue of the Americas, New York, New York 10020

This book is a memoir. It reflects the author's present recollections of her experiences over a period of years. Some names and identifying details have been changed and some dialogue has been recreated from memory.

SIMON & SCHUSTER BFYR is a trademark of Simon & Schuster, Inc.

For information about special discounts for bulk purchases, please contact Simon & Schuster Special Sales at 1-866-506-1949 or business@simonandschuster.com.

The Simon & Schuster Speakers Bureau can bring authors to your live event. For more information or to book an event, contact the Simon & Schuster Speakers Bureau at 1-866-248-3049 or visit our website at www.simonspeakers.com.

Also available in a SIMON & SCHUSTER BFYR hardcover edition

Book design by Lucy Ruth Cummins

The text for this book is set in Adobe Caslon Pro.

Manufactured in the United States of America

First SIMON & SCHUSTER BFYR paperback edition June 2015

4 6 8 10 9 7 5

The Library of Congress has cataloged the hardcover edition as follows:

Hall, Shyima.

Hidden girl : the true story of a modern-day child slave / Shyima Hall

with Lisa Wysocky.

pages cm

Audience: Grade 9 to 12

ISBN 978-1-4424-8168-8 (hardcover) — ISBN 978-1-4424-8170-1 (eBook)

1. Child slaves—Juvenile literature. 2. Child slaves—United States—Juvenile literature. 3. Child abuse—United States—Juvenile literature. 4. Foster parents—United States—Juvenile literature.

I. Wysocky, Lisa, 1957—II. Title.

HD6231.H35 2014

362.7'7—dc23

[B]

2013011860

ISBN 978-1-4424-8169-5 (pbk)

To Mark Abend, for helping me navigate life in the United States,
for his assistance in helping me raise awareness of basic human rights,
and for his dedication to ending slavery in our world.—S. H.

ACKNOWLEDGMENTS

I would first like to thank ICE (Immigration and Customs Enforcement) and the caring people there for rescuing me. If not for them, I might still be held in bondage. Thank you to Lisa Wysocky (my coauthor), Sharlene Martin (my literary agent), Zareen Jaffery (our editor), and our publisher, Simon & Schuster Books for Young Readers, for helping me tell my story. Last but never least, a big thank-you has to go to my loved ones—Athena, Daniel, Karla, Amber, Teresa, and PaNou—for the many times you showed me how much you love and care for me. I love you all.

—S. H.

Shyima Hall is a remarkable young woman who has overcome astonishing odds to become the strong, independent person she is today. I want to thank her for sharing her story intimately with me, and ultimately with you. Huge thanks to literary agent Sharlene Martin of Martin Literary Management, for always going the extra mile; to Special Agent Mark Abend for being diligent in confirming the details of Shyima's life; and to Daniel Uquidez, Amber Bessix, Teresa Bessix, and Karla Pachacki, who were all extremely helpful. To Zareen Jaffery and everyone else at Simon & Schuster Books for Young Readers: This book would not have become a reality without you. Human trafficking in the United States (and worldwide) is a serious and growing problem. Through Shyima, I hope you become more aware of this terrible practice and will share her story with others.

—L. W.

CHAPTER ONE

Everyone has a defining moment in his or her life. For some it is the day they get married or have a child. For others it comes when they finally reach a sought-after goal. My life, however, drastically changed course the day my parents sold me into slavery. I was eight years old.

Before that fateful day I was a normal child in a large family in a small town near Alexandria, Egypt. Growing up in a poor neighborhood in Egypt is nothing like life for kids in America. Like many who lived in the community I was raised in, our family was quite poor. I was the seventh of eleven children, many of whom were much older, and to this day I can't recall the names of all of my brothers and sisters.

We moved many times when I was a child, but the last home I lived in with my family was our downtown second-story apartment. It was tiny, just two rooms that we shared with two other families, and there was not room during the day for everyone to be inside. At night our family slept together in a single room, and the two other families shared the second room. Our family slept on blankets on the floor, as we weren't rich enough to have beds. There was one bathroom for everyone—including the people who lived in the other three units in the building.

I know my parents were happy once—I had seen photos of them laughing on the beach, and with their arms around each other, photos taken in the first years of their marriage. The parents I knew, though, didn't speak to each other. Instead, they yelled. And I never once saw them hold hands or embrace.

My dad worked in residential construction, possibly as a brick-layer, but he was often absent from our home for weeks at a time. When Dad did show up, he acted in a way that I now know is abusive. He was a loud, angry, belligerent, unreasonable man who beat us whenever he was displeased, which was often. My father eventually spent more and more time at his mother's, but this was not necessarily a bad thing, as life was calmer when he was not around.

Even though Dad beat us, there were good times with him too. A number of times he held me in his arms and told me how lucky he was to have me. It was during those times that I felt completely loved, and my own love for my dad would be strong.

But then he'd flaunt other women in front of us, and in front of my mother. Outside we'd see him flirting with women. Even as young as I was, I knew instinctively that was wrong. Plus, I could see the grim line of my mother's mouth and the sadness in her eyes. Unfortunately, in our neighborhood there were any number of women who thought nothing of spending private time with another woman's husband. Most of the men I saw acted just as my dad did. It is sad to me that that kind of behavior was accepted.

Every time my dad came home, I hoped he would be different, but he never was. I hated waking up in the morning to hear my parents fighting, and that's why I was never too unhappy when he left to go back to his mother's house.

I didn't like my father's mother, because she was as mean and bitter as he was. I did not know the rest of his family well enough to know if they were like that too. His family members did not like my mother and rarely came to see us. On the rare occasion when we visited his mother's home, my grandmother asked him in front of us about other women that he spent time with, and she made it a point to tell us how awful our mother was, even when our mother was present. I never understood that, because my mother was our rock. She was the backbone of our family and was the person who made sure we had what few clothes and food that we did have.

I don't know why my mother married my dad. Neither of their families approved of the match, but in the early years they had a good life near my mother's family in Alexandria. They had a nice home, four children, and were in love. Then an earthquake hit, and everything they had was reduced to rubble.

My mom and dad did not have the mental strength to move

on from that level of disaster, for they never got their lives back together after that. Life began to spiral downward, and by the time I came along on September 29, 1989, my family was living in poverty in a slum.

When I was young, my mother was constantly sick, tired, and pregnant. I was later diagnosed with rheumatoid arthritis (RA), when I was in my teens, and I think my mother may have had it too, because genetics play a big part in who ends up with RA.

Rheumatoid arthritis is a long-term autoimmune disease that causes inflammation of the joints and surrounding tissues. Wrists, fingers, knees, feet, and ankles are most commonly affected, but RA can affect organs, too. The disease begins slowly, usually with minor joint pain, stiffness, and fatigue. Morning stiffness is common, and joints may feel warm, tender, and stiff when not used for a while. It is not an easy disease to live with, and it must have been even harder for my mother, who had few resources and who had to care for her many children.

In Egypt many children do not go to school. It is legal there for children to stop school and begin work when they are fourteen years old. Only families that need money force their children to begin working at that age, but the families that struggle the most don't send their kids to school at all. We were one of those families. I never went to school and never learned to read or write. (I did both much later in life, after I was freed.) I had four younger siblings, and my role in the family was to care for them while my parents worked.

To my knowledge only one of my sisters ever attended school.

She was the fourth child in our family, and my mother's parents were raising her. Except during holidays, I never saw her. This sister led a completely different life from the rest of us. She even went to college, which was unheard of for people of our status in Egypt. I am not sure why this sister lived with our grandparents, but it might be because she was the youngest of my parents' four children when the earthquake hit. Maybe my grandparents offered to take her temporarily to help out while my parents got back on their feet, and it turned into a more permanent arrangement.

The two oldest of my siblings were twin girls. One twin left early on to get married, and I never saw much of her after that. It was as if she'd jumped at her first opportunity to escape our family. The other twin, Zahra, was the wild child in our family. She was always getting into trouble, which may have been why my parents sent her to work for a wealthy family who lived several hours away.

When it came to my brothers, I'm not sure what they did. I know that some of my older brothers went to school, because they got up every morning, gathered their books, and walked to the school that was not too far from our house. At least I think that's what they did most days. Other days they could have had jobs or have been carousing on a street corner somewhere. I wish I had thought to ask my brothers to teach me to read and write, but for whatever reason, that thought never came into my head.

My oldest brother, Hassan, was born between the twins and the sister who lived with our grandparents, and I know his name because it was the surname that I was born with. I was born Shyima El-Sayed Hassan, and my brother was Hassan Hassan. "El-Sayed" was my mother's maiden name, and it was common practice in Egypt then to use the mother's maiden name as a child's middle name. I am sorry to say that while I can guess, I am not 100 percent sure about the names of my other siblings.

I do know that the two siblings who came between the sister who lived with our grandparents and me were boys. They were my brothers, but I didn't like them much. I was too young to know much about Hassan, but these two boys were turning out to be much like our father. They were rude, loud, and demanding, but what I recall most about them was that when they paid any attention to me, the attention consisted of inappropriate touching.

No one had ever talked to me about not letting others touch my private parts. In fact, I wasn't even sure it was wrong when my brothers did. I am not sure when it started, maybe when I was around five or six. The touches made me feel bad inside, and I avoided the boys whenever I could. I never knew if my mother knew what the boys were doing, but I think that she didn't. I didn't tell her, because I didn't know it was wrong. Familial relationships were murky to me, and I didn't know anything about appropriate boundaries.

Since then I have wondered if, after I left, they touched any of my younger sisters as they had me. My older sisters were old enough—and not around enough—to not let them get away with that. At least I hope that is the case. But that is the thing about abusers: They choose vulnerable people.

There was a time, however, when one of my brothers saved me. I was about seven, and we had been playing on some hay bales that were stacked near our apartment. I didn't have any shoes on, and when I jumped off the stack of hay onto the ground, I landed on the edge of a sheet of glass and cut off all the toes on my right foot. I must have been in shock; I didn't even notice until another kid said, "Hey, what happened to your foot?" There was little blood at that point. Sometimes when amputations occur there is so much shock to the body that the body draws blood away from the area for a time. Apparently that is what happened to me.

One of the oddest things about this story is that I was not freaked out. After the accident I went around and picked up my toes. Then a neighbor kid grabbed me and carried me to my brother, who put me in a litter-type carrier. A litter is a large fabric sling that has long poles attached to the sides that extend in front of and behind the sling. Two people, one in front and one behind, stand between the poles and pick them up. Then the people carry the litter as they run to a destination. This was a common type of transportation in our town.

Nothing hurt until the people carrying the litter began to head to the hospital. Then the blood started to flow and I became petrified with fear and pain. The only things I recall of the hospital itself are the bed I lay on and that the bed was in an enclosed room, rather than being in the open. But the surgery to reattach my toes stays in my mind, as they did it without any anesthesia. You can imagine how painful that was! A nurse held my squirming body down as the doctors worked on my foot. Their faces were masked, which meant all I could see of them was the concern in their eyes.

I was terrified that I would die. The pain of the procedure was far greater than anything I had ever experienced, and after, when I saw the scary amount of my blood on the surgical towels that had been used during the operation, I thought I might faint.

Right after the operation I went home, although I am not sure how I got there. Then I stayed off my foot for a long time. When I started walking again, my dad said, "Do you want to lose your toes again? They are not healed. Sit down." That his words have stuck in my head must mean that he was home for part of that time. I know that my mom changed the wrap on my foot several times. I must have gone back to a doctor to get the stitches removed, but I do not remember any of that. Today I have all of my toes, but only two of them work normally—my big toe and the toe next to it.

My life in Egypt was like that—simple happiness interrupted by unimaginable tragedy. It was an unsafe world. But it was my home.

While I never connected with my older brothers and sisters, I adored my younger siblings. Closest in age to me was a boy, then a girl and another boy, then my baby sister. When the first three of my four younger siblings were born, a midwife came, and the rest of us were sent out of the one room we lived in. But my youngest sister came into this world on a day when my mother and I were in our apartment while the rest of our family had gone to visit relatives to celebrate a holiday. When my youngest sister was born, my mother lay on a blanket while I guided the baby's head out. My mother instructed me to pull the head, but not too hard. I think my attachment to this younger sister was strong because I was there during her birth.

After my sister was born, my mom said, "Go down to the neighbors, and one of the women there will come to help." That was a big thing, because most of the people in our neighborhood were mean to my mother. I think between my mother's unsuccessfully trying to correct my brothers' behavior and having eleven children, other people looked down on her. And, as she behaved with my dad, my mother never stood up for herself with the neighbors. Instead she just took their verbal abuse. She forgave people all the time and often said, "You can't stay mad at people."

I hated that my mother allowed others to treat her poorly, and I wondered if she allowed people to steamroll her at work, too. My mother never said much, and when she did, she was soft-spoken. It was not in her nature to be mean. Instead she took the negative behavior people dished out to her.

As for my older brothers and sisters, they were away from our home for long periods of time. My mother might have been in contact with them when they were gone, but if so, she never mentioned it to me. I might not see a family member for months (or years), and then one day, poof, there they were. When I got to see my older sisters on holidays, especially the sister who was being raised by my grandparents, I was glad to see they were stronger women than my mother was. Holidays were about the only days I got to interact with my older sisters, and I paid close attention to what they said and did. I hoped that someday I could find that kind of strength for myself. Little did I know that I would need it sooner rather than later.

Though my family moved many times, each place we lived in was much the same. Each home was in a run-down two- or three-story apartment building in the middle of town, with anywhere from four to twelve units in the building. Once, we were kicked out of an apartment in the middle of the night for failure to pay rent.

"Gather your things," my mother said, and we did. There wasn't much. That night my mother, my two older brothers, all of my younger siblings, and I slept in the street because we had no car and nowhere to go. The next day we walked what seemed like forever until we got to another apartment that was much like the last.

I can look back now and see how hard that must have been on my mother. With the continual pregnancies—close to a dozen children—and her being ill, the many moves added to the stress of her life. My mother was well spoken, and I believe that she was an educated woman. I know that she had a job, but if I ever knew what she did, I have long forgotten.

One day my mother tried to enroll me in school. I must have been no more than seven years old at the time. I don't know what motivated her to do that, but I was excited about the possibility.

My older sister who lived with my grandparents went to school, and she was smart. I wanted to be just like her. But, when we got to the school, we were told that I was too old. Too old? How can seven be too old to go to school? It may have been that there was no room at that particular school, or that it was during the middle of the school year and they didn't want to add a new student right then, but the result was that I cried for the rest of the day.

Since then I have met a lot of kids who complain about having to go to school. What if they never had the opportunity to get an education? What if they never learned to spell or count, or never learned anything about history or geography? How would these people who complain about going to school get through life?

Not being able to go to school broke my heart, and I was jealous that my brothers had the opportunity to learn. I was jealous of the entire process, from getting up in the morning and getting dressed, to them coming home in the afternoon to do their homework. Knowing that I would not have the chance to be part of this left me dejected for days. The only thing that pulled me out of it was my younger brothers and sisters.

From the time I was about five years old I was in charge of our apartment while my mother worked during the day. I helped my mother with the daily tasks of the household: sweeping, washing, cooking, and overseeing my two younger brothers and the first of my younger sisters. My younger siblings were everything to me. They were my world, and I loved them from the bottom of my heart.

Our mother was often gone all day, and when that happened, she locked us in our one room of the apartment. Then we might play dress-up. We used my mother's clothes and the clothes of my older sisters, although I'm not sure they ever knew this. We often played hide-and-seek under the blankets on the floor. Or we might play "good guy, bad guy," which was our equivalent of cops and robbers.

I'm not sure why our mother locked us in, but I can make a guess. The neighborhood we lived in was not safe. We lived in a center section of town where there were stabbings or shootings every now and then. And from my earliest days I knew not to speak to strangers. The streets were often busy, and there was the usual noise and activity that occurs when many people live close together. Some of that activity was unsavory, and when our mom thought the neighborhood was unsettled and something might happen, she locked us in. Our neighborhood was small, and news traveled fast. If we knew something like that was going on, we stayed inside. On some days when we were playing outside, friends or neighbors suggested that I get my siblings off the street. Then I'd hurry to round them up and take them to our apartment. On safer days we hung out outside, played games on the street, and moved to the side only when a car came by.

When I wasn't playing with my brothers and sisters, I kept busy cooking and cleaning. I washed our clothes by hand in a bucket. It was a lot of work, but I washed only the clothes that were abso-lutely filthy, and it helped that none of us had much to wear. I usually had whatever I was wearing, plus a T-shirt and pants, and then a dress for holidays. All of our clothes were hand-me-downs, and by the time the clothes got to me, they were pretty worn. But I didn't mind. No one in our neighborhood had a lot; I was no different from anyone else I knew.

We usually had food for dinner, but not always. When we had food, it was rice or bread, and once in a while, meat. If there was money for a few potatoes, we went to a market some distance away to get them. When we got home, my mom would boil the potatoes and we'd share them for dinner. On a good day my mother would make a special recipe of grape leaves stuffed with rice. (Recipe in the back of the book!) Even though my mother often had to modify it because we did not have all of the ingredients, this was a treat!

Most days we ate two meals, and occasionally we might have had fruit or vegetables similar to those eaten here in the United States. I do know that I felt hungry during much of my childhood.

While I was glad to have food, I was even happier on the rare occasions when I got to take a shower. We had only one bathroom for the four apartments in our building, so bathing was not a regular thing. Our bathroom had to be shared by more than twenty people, and a portable heater warmed our water. On top of that we had to have money to buy oil to heat the water and had to carry all of our water, including our drinking and bathing water, from a well that was a long distance from our apartment. This was because we had no running water. For those reasons no one took long showers, although I often had to wait in a long line to use the toilet.

When we slept, we had a blanket under us and a blanket over us. There were no pillows and no designated sleeping places. That's why I always ended up sleeping in a different part of the room next to a different person. During summer months it got hot in that room, so hot that I could not sleep. I'd toss and turn, sticky with sweat, before getting up in the middle of the night to open our one window.

I wore the same clothes for sleeping that I wore during the day. There was no such thing as pajamas in our family, and most times the next day I'd wear the same clothes I had worn the day, and the night, before.

Then there was the rain. It seemed to me that there was a lot of it. And because our streets were not paved, the hard-packed dirt quickly turned to mud. There often were rivers of mud streaming down the street in front of our apartment. I hated that, because it meant I'd have more clothes to wash in my bucket and a lot more water to haul to wash the clothes in.

But I had some fun, too.

Some of my earliest remembrances are of playing marbles with my siblings out on the street. To play, we drew a circle in the dirt, or outlined a circle on the street with chalk. Then each of the players put some marbles inside the circle. When it was my turn, I'd take a slightly larger marble and try to knock some of the others out of the circle. Any marbles that I knocked out, I got to keep. I had a lot of marbles!

I also had a good time getting dressed up in my dress to visit relatives. These visits were usually with members of my mother's family. We had to visit secretly, though, as my dad forbade us to visit my mother's relatives. Often we went on the train to Alexandria and then walked a long way to my grandparents' house, but once in a while my uncle picked us up in his car. In either case, my mom would whisper to us, "Shhh. Don't say anything about this." We never did.

My maternal grandmother and grandfather were warm and loving, and their delight in seeing us was evident. There was always a lot of food and laughter when we visited. My grandmother was the most wonderful, caring lady, and my grandfather always gave us money for the candy store next door. When he passed away from complications related to alcoholism, I was saddened beyond anything I had ever known. I couldn't have been more than seven years old.

There were many aunts, uncles, and cousins whom we visited at my grandparents' house, although I no longer remember any of their names. We had many happy times there. When we visited, I felt as if everything was right in my world. And you know what? Everything *was* right. What it comes down to is that no matter how poor we were, how absent or abusive my father was, how hard I had to work, I was a happy child.

Despite our poverty, I was happy. I understand that some of that feeling was the unbridled joy of being a child, but the other reason for my happiness was love. Even though by American standards I was a neglected child, in those days I loved and was loved. It was all I knew. My younger siblings and I had formed an especially tight bond, and I adored looking out for them and being with them. Life was good.

CHAPTER TWO

My life with my family seems long ago, and my memories of that time feel far away. But there are details I will never forget. The way the dust flew up from the streets whenever a car passed, the feel of the hot dirt under my bare feet when I played outside, the sounds of the children in my neighborhood laughing, the way the colors on the clothes we hung outside to dry faded in the harsh sun.

That is the thing about memories of my early life. Some moments are etched into my mind clearly, and I see them in my mind as if they happened just yesterday. Other moments are fuzzy and vague, and yet others I have no recollection of. I have learned to hold close and treasure the positive memories and the good feelings they give me.

One day our entire household was in an uproar because one of my older sisters had been dismissed from her job in a shameful manner.

I was eight years old by this time, and my sister Zahra, one of the twins, had been working for some time for a wealthy man and his wife in Egypt's capital city of Cairo. Our town near Alexandria was several hours north and west of Cairo by car, and after Zahra went to work in Cairo, I did not see her much. Not that I had seen her much before. Zahra was quite a bit older than I was—when I was eight, she could have been anywhere from sixteen to twenty, or maybe even older—and the age difference between us, and her frequent absences from our home, had made bonding next to impossible.

My parents had arranged for Zahra to work for this family, and while she had been paid a pittance (which my mother had picked up every month), she'd technically been held in bondage. I later learned that Zahra had never had days off, had not been able to leave the home of her employers unescorted and without permission, and had had to endure all sorts of physical and verbal abuse. My sister had essentially worked from sun up to sun down.

In Egypt it is not unusual for a poor family to make a contract like this with a richer family. I think the contract my parents made with this family said that Zahra was supposed to work for them for ten years, and she was into the contract for only two or three years when she was "fired." When we learned Zahra had been dismissed, there was a lot of yelling. And on this day my father's yells were exceptionally irate.

A few days later my mother, my youngest sister, and I went to visit Zahra's former employers in Cairo. I was the oldest girl living at home, so I often traveled with my mother. Most of the travel was to the market or to help her with errands near our apartment. But my baby sister and I had occasionally accompanied our mother when she'd go to pick up Zahra's "pay." On a few of those trips I saw the family's twin boys, who were younger than I was, and their youngest daughter, who was about my age.

Few things stick in my mind from our trip to see Zahra's former employers, but I do know that I stood in the enormous bedroom of the woman of the house as I held my baby sister. I could not have loved that little girl more if she had been my own child. I am sad to say that I no longer recall her name.

On that day there was another lady in the room. I came to understand that Nebit was a relative of the employer family, and that her family lived in that huge house too. The first woman was lying in her bed, and she told my mom that my sister had stolen money from them. More than my family could ever pay back. My mother had already confirmed this fact with my sister and knew the accusation to be true.

"You can't pay back what your girl stole," said the lady in Arabic. "So you can either provide us with someone else to work to repay the debt or we'll call the police."

Tears leaked from my mother's eyes. I stood, silent, holding back my wild emotions. I felt afraid of this lady's threat, and sad for my mother's tears.

Then the woman said, "I can train the young one from the ground up, and we won't have these adult issues of stealing."

From what I could gather from the rest of the conversation,

the contract my parents had made with this family was that my sister was supposed to have lived in this home and helped with the cooking and cleaning. Then I heard my mother agree that the fair thing for everyone was for another girl to work in Zahra's place.

"All right. It's a deal," the woman said in Arabic.

The pit of my stomach lurched when I realized the girl they were talking about was me.

Then my mother began to talk about me as if I were nothing more than a piece of furniture, a commodity. How could she talk about me in this callous manner? Didn't she love me anymore? A black hole formed in the core of my being as I realized I was going to have to leave my mother, my siblings, my home, my life. I had rarely been outside of my neighborhood and had certainly never been around strangers this far from home. I was confused and began to cry hard enough to shake my whole body.

When we are young, it often is the emotion of an experience that stays with us the longest. A child might not remember the details of a bad dream, but the feeling of terror the dream brings can remain for a lifetime. That's how that day is for me. The feeling of abandonment is almost as fresh today as it was fifteen years ago, when I was eight. I had not had much experience in life, but I knew that families were supposed to stick together. Parents were supposed to nurture and support their children, not sell them to strangers.

I have spent many hours wondering about my parents' motivation. While Zahra had been earning a tiny amount of money every month that had gone to my parents, my employment in the house would be for the sole purpose of paying off her debt. This was not just the debt from the money she'd stolen; it was a debt of honor. My sister had caused this family grief, and to make up for that I was expected to become their domestic slave.

Why did my mother not say no? Why did she not fight for me? I was eight! Were we so destitute that my family could no longer feed me? Did my mother think my prospects were better living with this woman and her family as their slave than they would be if I lived at home? Was our family "honor" that much more important than I was? Had my parents been told the truth about what my position in the home would be? Did my father even care for me? Why did he allow this?

In recent years I have had a lot of therapy to better deal with the issues these questions have raised, and I have mostly made my peace with what happened. But on that day, when I was an eight-year-old child, I felt thrown away, and I was terrified that I would never see my home again. Unfortunately, I was right.

My mother hugged me tightly before I said a sad good-bye to my baby sister. My mother's final words to me were "Be strong."

On one hand, I could not believe she was leaving me there. On the other, I held out hope that I was going to stay for only a few days, a week at the most. In either case I felt betrayed. I was too young to understand that slavery was not an unusual situation for Egyptian families of our lower economic status. For my parents, for this family, this was part of life.

With tears falling down my face, I looked out the window as my mother walked down the long driveway with my beloved baby sister. I wanted to savor every last drop of my family, so I watched until my mother turned a corner and I could no longer see her.

Neither my mother nor I knew when we walked into that house that day that I would not return home with her. Because of that I had nothing with me. No clothes, not even a familiar blanket or a photo of my family. I had nothing, and I was devastated.

I never learned what happened to Zahra after I left, but I imagine that my father beat her—that is, he may have if she ever came home when he was there. It is possible that she did not see him for some time, or that she was sold to someone else. I'm fairly certain she was an adult by this time, though, and may have had more options. However, in the aftermath of her theft, Zahra was "tainted goods," which would have made "employment," or marriage to a quality man, difficult. Plus, the reason Zahra had been sold into slavery in the first place might have been because she was the family troublemaker. Maybe my mother and father had misguidedly thought it would settle her down and help her grow up. Or maybe they'd valued the money their child produced more than they'd valued the child.

I don't know if Zahra stole money from the family because she'd planned to run away and escape her bondage, or if she stole it because she knew that the act would cause her to be returned to our family. I tend to think the first scenario holds the truth, but I may never know for sure.

These unanswered questions are typical of my life, and of the lives of many children (and adults) who are held in bondage. Slaves often lose track of family and places, and memories fade or become distorted. Unfortunately, there are thousands of us—children and adults who live their lives in slavery in Egypt, Europe, and even in the United States.

According to the United States Department of Health and Human Services, human trafficking is the fastest-growing criminal industry in the world today. There are two different forms of human trafficking: in one a person is recruited under false circumstances, and in the second a person is sold without his or her knowledge or consent. The latter is what happened to me, and is slavery in its truest sense. A few years ago I was stunned to learn from a 2005 Trafficking in Persons Report by the State Department in Washington that as many as eight hundred thousand people are trafficked across international borders every year. Half of those victims are believed to be children.

Most people think slavery in the United States was stamped out during the Civil War, but that's not true. Legalized slavery is gone, but today as many as 17,500 people who are held in bondage are illegally brought into our country every year. And it is estimated that there are more than forty-three thousand slaves in the United States at any given time. Even worse, there are as many as twenty-seven million slaves globally.

In the United States only about 2 percent of those who are held in bondage are eventually rescued. I find that number appalling, but it is a higher percentage than in other countries. Many of the rescues here come through tips that neighbors give to their local police departments. A neighbor has a feeling something is not quite right next door, and after long deliberation they finally call.

But in Cairo there was no nosey neighbor, and no one called. No one knew I was there, because the estate these people lived on was huge and the mansion was far away from other houses. A few days, or maybe a week, after my mother left me in the home of these strangers, my new cruel reality began to dawn on me on a deeper level—that I was not going home. Ever. I became hysterical and insisted that someone call my mother and tell her to come pick me up.

That was difficult for several reasons. First, my family did not have a telephone. Second, my captors, as I came to think of the man and his wife, were not about to call my mother. Instead I pleaded with and enlisted the help of some of the other people who worked in the house. There were several, all adults, who worked and lived in the household in various capacities, and they were kind to me. It took some time, but eventually I found my mother on the other end of the phone line. I was so happy to hear her voice that I was probably incoherent. But the tone of her voice shattered me.

"You are good. You do good for our family. You must stay there," she said. "If you do not, bad things will happen to you."

I could barely breathe. My mother had truly abandoned me. Didn't she want me? How had this happened? What had I done to deserve this? Of course the answer was: nothing. I had done nothing but be a happy young girl who loved her family. I found that for me the old saying "bad things sometimes happen to good people" was true.

When I hung up the phone, I turned around and looked at my coworkers in dismay. This life of slavery, of bondage, was going to be my life. Forever. I crumpled to the floor and sobbed.

It turned out that I was not held in bondage forever, although every day I was a slave was a day too many. I was one of the lucky ones; I was one of the fortunate 2 percent. I was rescued, but that wouldn't happen for a number of years. First I had many tears to shed. I had to find inner resources that I didn't know existed, and I would have to travel halfway around the world before the freedom I longed for was mine.

Every day when I woke up in the home of my captors, the first thing I thought of was the home and beloved family I had left behind. And, whenever I had a free moment during the day—which wasn't often—my family popped back into the forefront of my mind.

I'd had many friends in our neighborhood. I had loved my mother, my younger siblings, our neighbors, and my extended family. I had loved my life and my sense of belonging, and I hated that when I was sent to live with my captors, my parents allowed all that to be taken away.

CHAPTER THREE

Abdel Nasser Eid Youssef Ibrahim and his now former wife, Amal Ahmed Ewis-abd Motelib, were my captors. I addressed them as sir and ma'am, as I was not allowed to call them by their names, but in private I did not give them that kind of respect. Instead I thought of them as The Mom and The Dad. They called me "stupid girl."

I would soon realize that The Mom always had a sour expression on her face. Nothing anyone ever did was good enough for her. She was always displeased, and always entitled. The Dad was on the phone so much, I am surprised it did not attach itself permanently to his ear. He always argued with whomever he was talking to, and his eyebrows knitting together accompanied his angry voice. He also touched his forehead often in an effort to help himself relax. In retrospect, his face was not anywhere near as mean as his wife's.

My captors wore Western-style clothes, and by that I do not mean cowboy clothes but clothes that the average person would wear here in the United States. For them it was all about the brand. If a specific exclusive designer would impress other people, those were the clothes that they wore.

The Mom and The Dad and their five children lived in a five-story, gated, brick home on sprawling grounds. I thought the house looked like a castle. I did not go out of the house much, but when I did, each time I was amazed at the size of the property. To get there you would turn off the main road onto a long drive and pass several houses that were spaced far apart. These were houses for groundskeepers and others who were employed on the estate. You'd then pass a large and beautiful garden that looked like something you'd see in a famous painting.

The main house had a seventeen-car garage and an elevator, and on the first floor was an indoor pool with a retractable roof that opened to the sky. The family accessed the pool from either the elevator or a broad set of stairs, but I had to use a separate staircase, one that descended from the kitchen and was reserved for the help.

The rest of the first floor was furnished to impress guests and was filled with expensive sofas, chairs, and tables, with luxurious lighting and lots of knickknacks. Except for using the pool, none of the family hung out on the first floor, and the children of the family were specifically banned from the area. Instead, The Dad rented the space out to film companies and to corporations that held big parties and other events there.

The second floor held several large bedrooms. The Mom's brother and his wife and kids had rooms there, and the master bedroom was large enough to be a house by itself. There was a huge round bed in the middle of the room, with a sitting area by a large window. The master bathroom had two bathtubs and what seemed like acres of marble.

My captors had five children, and the two youngest were identical twin boys who were about five when I came into the household. The boys had a cute Winnie-the-Pooh–themed room on the second floor, with bunk beds; and the youngest daughter, who was close to me in age, had a beautiful Barbie-decorated room. To me it looked like a room a princess might sleep in.

Also on the second floor was a humungous kitchen that came fully equipped with a staff person who cooked for the family. The stairs that I was allowed to use to go from floor to floor were accessed from a corner of the kitchen.

The two oldest daughters slept on the third floor. The oldest had a weird totally black room with black walls and black carpet, while the second daughter had a room complete with posters that could have been any teen girl's room here in the United States.

Also on the third floor was a fully-equipped game room, and two huge sitting areas with televisions. The laundry facilities were on this floor too, which meant I spent a lot of time there. The fourth floor was reserved for guests and was rarely used, while the servants, myself included, slept on the fifth floor.

All of this was a culture shock for me. I couldn't believe homes and furnishings like this existed, and it was hard for me to fathom that people could live in such luxury.

A home like this required a small army of servants. There were four or five of us who lived in the house and cared for the family, but most of the others lived in separate servants quarters on the estate, or came in for the day. Each of us had different "employment" arrangements. Some servants worked for a small salary, while others had room and board as part of their compensation. These servants were not slaves and could return to their homes and families when they were not working.

Those of us who lived at the house slept in bunk beds in one of two rooms on the fifth-floor attic level. Some of these people were live-in maids, while others might have been indentured servants, or were being held in bondage, like me. Unfortunately, none of the other servants thought it odd that I was enslaved with this family. It is sad that child bondage was, and still is, common enough in Egypt that most people did not think too much about it.

My life in the mansion was strange in many ways that you might not imagine. This was the first time I had ever slept in a bed, the first time I ever had a pillow, and those were novelties unto themselves. (Not that I got to enjoy sleeping much.) Next to the two servant bedrooms there was a fairly large bathroom with two sinks, a bathtub, and a separate shower.

Even though the family ate from beautiful dishes and used nice silverware, the servants always ate from paper plates, drank from red plastic cups, and used cheap plastic silverware. It was never said, but it was always implied that we were not good enough to use the family's dishes.

The same went for the furniture. I was never told not to sit on any of it, but I never did because I knew I wasn't supposed to. On the rare occasion when I had more than a second to sit down during the day, I sat on a bench that was reserved for servants in the kitchen. Whether it was calculated or not, all of this combined to make me feel "less than," and isn't that how captors hope their slaves will feel? To complete the shredding of my self-esteem, I was never given any shoes to wear. Granted, everyone went barefoot inside the house, a common custom in that part of the world, but my only shoes were hand-me-down flip-flops.

Two of the women who lived in as servants were probably in their thirties. These women both had families—husbands and children—wherever home was for them. For various reasons they had fallen on hard times and worked as live-in help for The Mom and The Dad. Only on rare occasions did they go home to see their families.

The two ladies were nice and helped me a lot, especially in the first few months. I felt comfortable with them because they looked and dressed like my older sisters. In that way these two ladies reminded me of home. It is typical for Muslim women to have their hair covered with the traditional head covering, the hijab. This is a veil that covers the hair and neck and is worn in public—and in the presence of unrelated adult men—and these women covered their hair.

There was also a mother and her daughter working as servants. The daughter must have been about twenty, and didn't want to be there. I can't blame her. I didn't want to be there either. Turnover for many of the workers was high, and some stayed only a few days. There must have been several dozen of these workers who were in and out quickly during the years I was there.

We were all busy and rarely got to talk to one another during the day. At night we were too exhausted, but there was always some kind of discussion going on in the kitchen about the family— usually about The Mom and how snobby she was. I did not participate much in these discussions, but I listened a lot. It gave me comfort to know that my fellow servants and slaves felt exactly the same way about the family that I did.

The Mom's attitude wasn't the only thing that bothered people. The Dad had a bad temper. If someone displeased him, his first reaction was to slap them. If he was very angry, he'd take off his belt and give them a few whacks with it. This included not only the servants in the home but also his wife and children.

I had a lot of trouble adjusting from being the young girl who lived happily in a large impoverished but loving family, to living in a home where I was demeaned every day in hundreds of ways. Being called "stupid girl" was the least of it. There were never enough hours in the day to do all of the work that was assigned to me—even though the family had a newer vacuum and other cleaning supplies for me to use. Early on, every night I'd cry what seemed like a year's worth of tears. How could my mother have abandoned me to this kind of life? I never understood how she—how any mother—could subject a child she loved to this. I know that to my dying day I never will understand it.

Working in the home, every day was the same. If I was not already up before dawn, one of the other servant ladies would wake me, even though I was exhausted from the day before. Then I'd hurry downstairs to the kitchen, where another lady gave me my assignments for the day. I didn't have to worry about getting dressed, because I usually wore whatever I had slept in. And, as when I'd lived with my family, I slept in what I had worn the day before. I often had a single change of clothes, but not always.

I never ate breakfast, even though one of my first jobs for the day was to help clean the kitchen. There simply was no time to eat, as the pace was brutal. When I was done and the dishes were put away, I cleaned the second-floor bathrooms. Then on the third floor I cleaned the television area and the game room. Those rooms were always the messiest because that's where the family hung out the most.

There were phones and intercoms throughout the house. (That's how the family communicated with one another most of the time.) And midday every day The Mom called her food orders down to the kitchen for the cook to prepare.

Most of my day was spent on the third floor, and I continued to be amazed at the immense size of two paintings that hung on the wall there. One painting was of The Dad, and the other was of The Mom. *Who does that?* I thought. Who would hang enormous paintings of themselves in their home? Even at that young age I thought it was ridiculous.

I did my best to clean everything spotlessly, because if The Mom didn't think a rug or a sink looked perfectly clean, I had to redo it. That took time I didn't have, and my negligence might earn me a slap. Between my regular duties I had to stop everything to bring family members whatever it was that they wanted, when they wanted it.

While I spent most of my day on the third floor, when I was done, I went back to help in the kitchen. A cook was there every day, but another of my jobs was to do the dishes. With a family of seven, plus the live-in relatives and their kids, over several meals throughout the day meant that there were several hundred dishes that I had to wash. The house had a huge dishwasher, but for some reason it was used only when visitors were there. There I'd be, dog tired, standing on a stool doing the dishes, because otherwise I was not tall enough to reach the counter or sink. It took forever.

Besides the dishwasher, there were many other fancy appliances that looked brand new. I'm not sure The Mom knew what each of them was supposed to be used for, and the cook stayed mostly with the traditional pots and pans for cooking.

Late evenings were the best part of the day because that was when I finally got to eat. I never ate, or even drank water, during the day, because I was too busy. By evening I was glad of the family's leftovers, and I ate as much as I could. I have to say that the quality of the food was better than what I'd had at home. While the family ate a lot of different dishes, usually what was left over after dinner was rice or meat. That's what I ate.

I filled my stomach, but it was never enough. I was soon hungry and remained that way until the next evening.

· · ·

I never thought about running away. Where would I go? I was miles and miles away from my family. The estate was gated, and I was far too small to get over the fence or the gate. Even if I made it to the main road, I wouldn't know which way to go. I was hours away from my small town. Then there was the promise from both my mother and The Mom that if I didn't cooperate, I would go to jail, where bad things would happen to me. I had no idea what those bad things might be, but life was already bad. I didn't want my life to be worse.

Instead of running away I rose early, every day, even though I had no alarm clock. But it would not have made much difference if I had, for I did not know how to tell time. I instead learned to gauge my day by the sun. If sunlight was streaming into the dining room window, for example, I knew the boys would be home from school soon. I also learned to mark time by the orders barked at me. "It's noon, stupid girl. Bring me a sandwich."

I rose early and on time most days, because I never slept well while I was with this family. That's because I was afraid. I kept a piece of me awake as a protective measure, because I never knew what The Mom or The Dad would do, or how they would act.

The Mom often did not rise until late morning, and The Dad was a businessman who did most of his business in one room of the house. I knew little about that, other than the bits and pieces of conversation I overheard while cleaning the house. I believe that he had inherited a steel business from his father. It was a big company, and all of his people came to him. Because of their schedules I did not interact with The Mom or The Dad much. Instead most of my contact with the family was with the kids.

The young twin boys I liked, and they seemed to like me, too. They had dark hair and dark skin and looked a lot like their mother. The two middle girls—the one my age and her next older sister, who was about thirteen—were both short with curly dark blond hair and took after their dad. They pretty much ignored me except when they wanted me to bring them a sandwich or re-iron a particular piece of clothing. The oldest girl was maybe fifteen and was the snobbiest of the kids. She was tall, dark-haired, and thin, like her mother.

When I did run into The Mom or The Dad, I tried to make myself invisible because I was terrified of them. Whenever they spoke to me, I stared at the floor. I had seen others in the household get slapped for looking The Mom or The Dad in the eye, and I didn't want that to happen to me. In that way the floor became my friend. In fact, I stared at the floor most of the time, even when the kids of the house were speaking to me.

The meanest person in the entire house, though, was Nebit. Several times I saw her push servants who had made the mistake of walking in front of her. She was a hateful person. And that is something that puzzles me to this day. These people had a large, beautiful home. They had an incredible indoor swimming pool and servants to take care of their every need. They had good food, beautiful clothes, and many fancy cars. But they were the unhappiest, most ungrateful people I have ever met. The Mom and The Dad were not happy with each other, and the kids had a huge sense of entitlement.

How could they not see how privileged they were? How could they not see how lucky they were to live that kind of lifestyle? Why couldn't they give thanks for their wonderful life or be appreciative of it? There are many things about my life then and the people in it that I did not understand. I probably never will.

Once or twice, though, I got to briefly speak with my mother on the phone. The calls were set up by The Mom and were mostly to discuss the details of payment for me to my parents. While I believed I had been paying off my sister's debt, as part of their deal with my parents The Mom and The Dad were paying them a small amount each month, the equivalent of seventeen US dollars. Later I learned that this arrangement was most likely a split—if, for example, my "employment" had earned me fifty dollars a month back in Egypt, The Mom and The Dad would have given my parents less, and the difference would have gone toward the debt my family owed. Every time I said, "Mom, I want to come home," my mother replied, "You are almost done. It's okay. You will be home soon." But even then I knew these for the placating words they were.

Plus, every time my mother and I spoke, either The Mom or The Dad listened in on another extension. Afterward, they'd yell at me. "You are a stupid girl," one or the other would shout. "You should be grateful for the good life we give you." It was like a broken record, or the movie *Groundhog Day*, where the same events take place over and over again.

Nothing was going to change of its own accord. I knew it and knew that the adults knew it.

CHAPTER FOUR

Life went on . . . and on. Day after day I waited on this family, took care of their every need, and cleaned their house. I took their verbal abuse and received more slaps than I care to count. I never had a day off, even when I did not feel well.

Every month it seemed someone had a birthday, or there was a Muslim holiday. I was never invited to participate, nor were my own birthdays celebrated. When the twins had their second birthday celebration since I'd been in the house, I knew I had been there a long time.

I had no knowledge of the calendar, of months or how years worked. Even though before I'd come to the home of my captors I had counted my age in years, I did not have a full concept of what that meant. Time was meaningless to me. Today was just a day—as was tomorrow.

I was too tired to be resentful. Too tired to be mad that other children were celebrating milestones and I was not. When you are a slave, it does not take long for your emotions to shut down or for your mind to go into survival mode. That may be why my memories of some occasions are spotty or nonexistent. My brain was on overload trying to survive, and day-to-day details were not necessary to that process.

But after I had been with my captors for a couple of years, I had the growing sense that this family had their own troubles. The Dad had been "away" a number of times for lengthy periods, and while nothing specific was said to me, I overheard conversations between family members or servants when they talked about him being in trouble with the law.

"He's coming home soon," the cook commented one day.

"*She* wants a big to-do when he gets home," added one of the maids.

"That'll be more work for us, mark my words," said another.

Just as some of the servants had predicted, when The Dad returned, there was a huge party. There were a lot of people at the party, so he must have had a lot of supporters.

Then there was a day when one of the servants left, then another. A short while later The Mom and the kids began packing their things, and I realized they were moving away because of work or personal trouble The Dad had. These goings-on were a major change from the sameness of my days, and I watched out of the corner of my eye with avid interest. I was excited! We were down to just a few servants who were helping close up the house.

Could this possibly mean I was going home? The thought was exhilarating; I barely dared to think about it.

I couldn't wait to see my family—especially my baby sister and my other siblings. It seemed like an eternity since I had last seen them. I didn't know if my family still lived in the same apartment, but I didn't care. If I could be with my family, it didn't matter if we lived in a hole in the ground.

One day not long after that The Mom said, "Your parents are coming tomorrow." I was so eager to see them! When my mother came, she gave me a hug, but both she and my dad arrived with cautious expressions on their faces. We all went right into the kitchen where The Mom said, "She is not yet done paying off her sister's debt. Our family is moving to the United States, and we need to bring one servant with us. That person will be the girl."

The girl, of course, was me. I had no concept of what this meant. I was ten years old, but I had never been to school. I didn't know what the United States was, or where it was. For all I knew it could have been a two-hour car ride away. But the distance didn't matter. I was devastated that I had to stay with my captors. Most of the other people who had worked or lived in the house had gone home to their families. Why couldn't I go too?

I was quite apprehensive about going to the United States. The only thing I had seen of it had been on the news. I didn't understand that it was another country, but I did realize that it was different from where I was now. Over the years my captors and their family and friends had often said what a bad place the US was, and I wondered with some unease why we were going there.

The Mom then handed my parents a pile of paperwork. "We will be gone only a few months," she said. Then I was asked to leave the room while my parents and The Mom talked further.

After my parents left, The Mom sent me out to have my hair cut. This was the first time I had ever been to a salon. In fact, I didn't even know such places existed. The experience was traumatic for me because my hair at this time was quite long and fell almost to my knees. After the haircut my hair came only to the middle of my neck. Then, because my hair is naturally curly, they chemically straightened it—possibly in an attempt to alter my appearance.

I cried and cried because I loved my hair. I didn't want to have it cut, but the lady at the salon had received instructions from The Mom, which meant I had no options. Back home The Mom saw my tears and told me to "get over it." Then she dressed me in a shirt that belonged to her youngest daughter. The shirt was red with tiny flowers on it. I never have liked the color red. Finally, I was introduced to a man named Aymen, who said, "Okay, let's go. Let's get started."

I had no idea what he meant. Get started for what? Where were we going? I was nervous when I left with him, but what else could I have done? My parents, The Mom, and now this man had tried to explain what was going to happen, but I had no concept of the ocean, airplanes, different countries, or customs other than what I knew in Egypt. My knowledge of life beyond my own was limited; there was no possibility of me understanding what was going on, other than that I knew I was not going home to be with my family. That's what I knew for sure, and for me that was the only thing that mattered.

Here I call the man by his first name, Aymen, but I think of him as "The Man That I Came With." First he took me to his house and showed me his daughter's room. The house was an average house, and the room was quite generic, as young girls' rooms go.

"When you get your passport, if you are asked anything, you are to describe this house, this room," he said. I didn't even know what a passport was.

Then we went to the home of a man who felt sneaky to me. I can't say why, exactly, other than that he had a dishonest vibe about him. I can no longer describe what he looked like, but I still sense the extreme unease I felt at this place. Aymen said to the man, "I am the girl's godfather and am in the process of adopting her." While the words were news to me, I didn't believe them. I knew Aymen said them so he could get what he wanted, which apparently was for the man to take my picture—after money changed hands. After some discussion Aymen handed the man more money and we left with a document that I later found out was a three-month visa to the United States. Aymen then took me back to the home of my captors.

Soon after that The Mom and the kids left for the United States. Several weeks passed during which The Dad, an older servant woman, and I were the only people in that huge, huge house. I began to wonder what was going to happen to me.

One day I was surprised to find my parents at the door. My mother packed my meager collection of clothing into a suitcase that had been obtained for me, and she added a photo of my family. Then my mom and dad spent the night with me on the fifth floor. I was thrilled that my mom and dad were there. Maybe we were going to stay together after all!

The next morning I got into a car with them and we went to the airport in Cairo. I had no idea what was going on. I didn't know I was permanently leaving the palatial home of my captors, or that I was going to fly halfway around the world. I also didn't have a clue that it would be the last time I ever saw my mom and dad.

Outside the airport, at the drop-off area for departing flights, we met up with Aymen.

"Good-bye," my mom and dad said. "We love you. We'll talk on the phone and we'll see you soon."

I never knew if my parents intentionally lied to me or if my captors had not told them the truth. I was leaving Egypt forever.

After a long flight Aymen and I landed in New York City. Aymen had not sat with me; he'd been in the front of the plane and I'd been in one of the last seats in the back. No one had taken the time to explain about flying to me. I had understood the concept. I had seen planes fly overhead before. But I hadn't known about the change in the cabin pressure as the plane rose into the sky, or that you could hear and feel the wheels clank as they slid back into the body of the plane. I had been bewildered during the flight, but hadn't known enough to be afraid.

Too, I hadn't expected the twenty-plus hours of travel time or the enormous size of the endless ocean. I didn't know how to read and had no toys to bring with me. With nothing to do, I'd soon fallen asleep. The entire experience had been too much to process and I had worn myself out.

After we landed in New York, Aymen and I transferred to another plane. On the way to the new gate, we walked past rows and rows of windows, but I barely noticed them. Instead I was overwhelmed with the bustle of the airport and the odd-sounding language that I later learned was English. And the clothes. I could not believe my eyes. I was astonished that women in the United States wore pants and also that they did not wear head scarves.

What most amazed me, though, were people of Asian descent. I had never seen an Asian person before. I didn't know any such kind of person existed. I had seen a few white people on the news when I had walked by one of the many television sets my captors had in Egypt, but the enticing, exotic look of people from China, Japan, and other Asian countries was a thing to wonder about. Being in the airport was like being dropped into an alternate universe, America was that much of a change for me.

Maybe I could have spoken up in the airport. Maybe I could have tugged on the pant leg of one of the scarfless women I passed and told them of my plight. But I spoke no English. I was afraid to leave Aymen's side because I had been told bad things would happen to my parents, brothers, and sisters if I didn't obey him. That's why I did not look for any kind faces in the airport, why I didn't tug on any pant legs. I was resigned. Resigned to go with the flow, resigned to this new country, resigned to a life of drudgery.

I can look back now and see how terribly wrong everything about my situation was. A ten-year-old girl should be bubbling and full of life. She should have masses of friends, learn important things at school, and be tucked into bed at night by a parent who loves her. I missed out on all of that. I guess it was a good thing that I didn't have any concept of what was lacking in my life.

The flight from New York to Los Angeles wasn't as long as the flight from Egypt to New York, but it seemed as if it were. I again sat in the back while Aymen sat in front. When we landed in California on August 3, 2000, I somehow knew we were done with the flying. I was glad of that, as the entire trip had taken almost a full day and night.

I had never learned about time zones, so I was doubly disoriented with jet lag and the change in time. Depending on whether daylight saving time is in effect, Cairo is either nine or ten hours ahead of Los Angeles. The flying time between Cairo and New York is almost twelve hours. The time spent getting to the airport, the two flights, and the wait time between the two flights meant I had been traveling for at least twenty-two hours.

Before we could meet up with The Mom and her oldest daughter, we had to go through customs. There, while we were passing through, a customs official looked at me oddly. He took an extra-long time with my passport and visa before he asked me a question.

Quietly Aymen said to me, "Smile." I smiled. Later I learned that Aymen had explained to the man that I did not speak or understand English. That much was true. Then he told the official, "I am adopting this girl and taking her to Disneyland."

I have wondered many times where life might have taken me if that customs official had questioned me, detained me, or sent me back to Cairo. Would I have ended up back with my family? Or would my parents have sent me back to my captors? If so, would my captors have tried again to get me into the United States? Of course I will never have answers to those questions, but for many years I batted those ideas around in my head.

My captors' new home was in an exclusive gated community in the city of Irvine, but it was nothing like the home they had left in Egypt. Instead of five floors this stucco home had only two. Instead of many acres, there was only a small lot. Rather than endless bedrooms, this home had only four: the master, a room for the two oldest girls, a room for the twins, and a smaller room for the youngest daughter. I slept in a tiny, windowless storage room in the three-car garage.

My room had a queen-size mattress that sat on a low metal frame. There was no place for my clothes, so they stayed in my suitcase. Because there was no heat or air-conditioning in the room, it was either uncomfortably hot or freezing cold. There was little air circulation, which made it hard to catch my breath, even when I left ajar the door that opened onto the garage. I have never seen any other house with that kind of setup in the garage, and I now wonder if my captors had the room built for me after they purchased the house and before I arrived.

At first there was a light in my tiny room, but after a few months the bulb burned out. I was far too short to replace it. The room was very dark after that. Lying there in the stuffy darkness became a thing for me to dread, and to this day I always leave a light on at night. Total darkness brings back to me those terrible hours I spent in the garage, and those are memories I would rather not have.

The Mom's relatives, Nebit and her husband, Sefu, lived in a house that was right next door. They had made the trip with my captor family, but there was no room for them in this house. Nebit came over almost every day, and she and The Mom spent a lot of time together, just as they had in Egypt. Nebit and Sefu did not have a servant of their own, so my job was to be sure both houses were kept spotless, as well as being a nanny for the twin boys.

When I first arrived, members of the family, including The Mom and The Dad, were somewhat kind to me. The kids were doing some regular chores, such as keeping their own rooms tidy. I was told that my only job was to clean all of the bathrooms. But what I was supposed to do and the scope of what I actually did were two different things.

In the morning I got up early, before anyone in the family. No one had ever given me an alarm clock, and in Egypt another servant had awakened me. Now I was expected to wake up on my own. I never slept well, but on the rare occasion when I wasn't up by dawn, one of the twins came to get me.

When I woke on my own, as I almost always did, I usually had to knock on the door that led from the garage to the house, as the family often locked that door at night. Having the door locked made it difficult for me, as I used a bathroom that was just inside the house, next to The Dad's office. If I had to use the bathroom in the middle of the night, I couldn't. I had to wait until morning.

Once both twins were up, I ironed the clothes they were going to wear to school that day. I made sure the twins got cleaned up, and then I woke the youngest daughter. After she had chosen her clothes for the day, I ironed those. Then I made their breakfasts—and their lunches—before I sent them out the door to school. It never crossed my mind that I should be going out that door with them. I was Shyima, the stupid girl, the slave.

By then the two older daughters, who were both in high school, would be up. My first words to them each morning were, "What can I do for you?" Then I ironed their clothes and made them a breakfast of coffee, juice, eggs, cereal, and bacon.

By this time I would have been interrupted at least a dozen times. One daughter would claim I hadn't ironed something right, and the other would ask me to hunt down her purse or her keys.

After the older girls left for school, I started on the downstairs. I first cleaned the family room next to the kitchen, because when

The Mom and The Dad finally got up, that was the first place they'd go. The Dad's office and bathroom were next, followed by two living rooms that no one used. But The Mom made sure I vacuumed and dusted them every day. She often said, "I didn't pay good money for the furniture to be dusty."

Right after noon The Mom and The Dad would get up. My first task when that happened was to run The Mom's bathwater. Then, before the twins got home in the afternoon, I had to pick up, dust, and vacuum four bedrooms *and* clean Nebit's house next door. The Mom and Nebit often had women they had met at their mosque over to The Mom's house. They didn't do much but chat away in Arabic (The Mom spoke no English and Nebit only a broken version), but when the women came over, everything had to be even more spotless.

The work was never ending. When I was in Egypt, I'd had the help of the other workers, but I was the only worker/slave my captors had brought to the United States. At ten years of age I had responsibility for all of it.

When the twins got home, I got their snacks ready, and because The Mom always wanted me to cook something, I started getting dinner ready. Only on rare occasions did she cook. When dinner was over, when the family was done eating, I could finally eat my single meal of the day.

Then it was time to get the boys ready for bed. I got their pajamas out and turned down their beds that I had made earlier in the day. I even put toothpaste on their toothbrushes. At midnight, long after the family members were asleep, I was still doing dishes and picking up the worst of their mess. Some nights I was up until two, three, even four in the morning. Then it started over again.

There were some variations to my routine, however. My captors often had visitors from Egypt. Most were family members, and when they arrived, the kids would double up in their bedrooms to free up space for the guests. Because it was such a long trip, the visitors usually stayed for longer than a weekend. While my captors were happy to see their relatives, it meant that I had that many more people to cook and clean for, that much more mess to pick up, that much more laundry to wash, iron, and dry. I was always glad when visitors left.

Sometimes the kids had friends over, and when that happened, I was told to stay in the kitchen out of sight. At first I thought the family was ashamed of me and didn't want to be embarrassed by me, but then it dawned on me that my captors knew that here in the United States my position in the household was not acceptable. That was brought home even more when, on occasion, I was told to hide in the pantry. I both liked and hated this bit of downtime, time when I could rest and relax, but I knew that the work I was responsible for still had to be done, knew that every minute I spent hidden away was another minute I would not sleep that night.

Another reason I hated the pantry was because there was no airflow in there. It was hot and stuffy, and I had to work to relax myself so I could breathe.

Even though I didn't like the time I spent in the pantry, I had a lot of motivation to go in there. At one point The Mom told me that if anyone outside the family or their visitors from Egypt saw me, I would be beaten, my family in Egypt would be beaten, and I would never see my family again. I soon learned to hide myself if others came into the house. Once in a while I didn't get hidden quickly enough, or I didn't know someone else was in the house, and a guest caught a glimpse of me. When that happened and people asked who I was, they were told that I was a cousin who was visiting from Egypt.

Despite all this, I was trusted enough to take the boys across the street to a small park. There was a slide and some swings among other playground equipment, and the twins, who were now about seven, had a great time there. I was not allowed to play, however, and instead had to sit on a bench and watch the boys. I wonder if my captors knew how odd that looked. I was ten, but I was small and looked much younger. I was a kid who should have been play-ing with the other children, but I couldn't remember the last time I'd played.

This was the first time I had ever been to a park. When I was with my family in Egypt, we played only in the streets or in vacant lots. I am not even sure if my area of Egypt had anything similar to a park.

The first time I took the boys was the first time I went outside my captors' home. It was quiet, and that surprised me. There were few cars on the road and even fewer people walking by. At my captors' home in Egypt I had expected the outdoor silence, because they'd lived on a great estate with no other buildings nearby, other than the servants' houses. My only other living experience had been in the middle of town, and there was always a lot of noise and activity there.

Sometimes moms or nannies who supervised other children who were playing asked about me. One lady in particular took special notice. She was a beautiful Asian woman, and after watching me for a time, she said something to me. I didn't speak English, so one of the twins said, "She is a sister from another mother. She lives in Egypt."

I was terrified, and my heart felt as if it were beating through my shirt. I didn't know if the lady suspected anything or not. While I wanted out of that household, my fear of what might happen to me—and to my family—if the lady said anything was so huge that I could barely breathe. I began to gather our things and asked the boys to come with me back to the house, but they weren't ready, they wanted to stay and play. With my heart still thumping, I gave them each a bottle of water and sat back down to wait for them.

The boys must have seen the long, speculative look the woman gave me and must later have said something to The Mom. After that we were allowed to go to the park only after The Mom glanced across the street and saw that no one else was there.

Next to the small park was a much larger park with a swimming pool. In the summer I often took the boys there to swim. The fact that I stayed on a lounge chair with the towels and food did not make me stand out, because many other people sat near the pool rather than going into it. The twins often invited me into the water, but I didn't know how to swim, and I was sure that The Mom and The Dad wouldn't approve.

I did not have any "nice" clothes to wear to the pool, and I was always somewhat self-conscious about how dirty my clothes were. Once in a while I caught people looking at me with odd expressions on their faces, and that made me feel bad. I still didn't speak any English, although I had picked up the stray word or two from the twins and from observing other kids at the park and at the pool. "Hi" was one of those words. I often wondered how I would get help for the twins if something happened, because I couldn't convey the nature of an emergency to anyone. I then debated what I would say if anyone approached me. But no one ever did. Everyone was too busy. They were excited about the pool and didn't pay any attention to me. I didn't know if that was a good thing or not.

Because I could not understand any of the conversation around me at the pool, I began studying people—the way they walked, their body language, the way they interacted with one another. Even though I was ten, my interactions with groups of people had been limited. With my biological family I'd mostly interacted with my younger siblings and my mother. With my captors I rarely saw anyone outside the near or extended family. That's why going to the pool became such a fascination for me.

From my chair I'd often glance away from the twins' antics in the pool to watch how teenage girls were with one another. I'd watch as a boy and a girl walked together, to try to find out if they were brother and sister, friends, or boyfriend and girlfriend. I watched older women, couples, and the lifeguards—who were, in actuality, older teens in a position of some authority. I watched grandmothers, people of different races, and young children.

While relationships between people were still somewhat of a mystery to me, those trips to the pool went a long way in developing my social skills. Even though I could not communicate verbally with anyone who did not speak Arabic, I could now better understand what people were saying with their eyes, their smile, the way they walked, and how close they stood to the person next to them.

These trips to the park and to the pool were fun for the boys, but I was still expected to get my work done. On days when I took the boys out, I worked far past midnight. If I ever thought that my duties would be lessened because of the boys' activities, I was wrong. I never brought this up to The Mom or The Dad, though, because I didn't want to be yelled at or, worse, slapped. My feelings didn't count, never counted. I was just Shyima, the stupid slave. I didn't exist.

CHAPTER FIVE

One day I came down with a terrible upper respiratory infection. I don't know if it was a bad cold, the flu, or strep, but I felt miserable. I had a high fever, I was coughing, my nose was running, my entire body ached, and I was weak and light-headed. I told The Mom I wasn't well, but she just said, "Oh, everyone gets that" and dismissed my concern.

I had nothing to compare this illness to, and no one to tell me any different. That's why I didn't think too much about it—until the next day. The next day I felt far, far worse. By day two I had no voice and it hurt to swallow. Imagine this, on top of my other symptoms. Plus I was wheezing and congested and had an even higher fever than the day before. But I was still expected to do all that I did every day. The Mom didn't allow me any downtime, which meant no time to rest and recover. Not only that, but The Mom refused to acknowledge that I was sick and denied me any medication such as an antihistamine, aspirin, or cough syrup.

I began to cry. There was no one to support me, to guide me, and because I had never been this sick before, I didn't understand what was going on with my body. Since I had begun living with my captors, I had been careful to always toe the line. I wanted to do the best job I could, because I was continually threatened with harm to my biological family—and with beatings and jail time for me—if I were not the perfect little slave. In fact, I was so afraid of getting into trouble for some small, unintentional infraction that I regularly got the shakes—especially when The Mom was around.

Now that I was extremely sick, however, I knew that if I were going to help myself, I had to be brave and step outside my tightly wrapped boundary. I also understood that I had to be sneaky about it. From previous family illnesses, I knew The Mom kept medicine in a big cabinet in her bathroom. I, of course, could not read Arabic, much less English, which meant I didn't know what the different medicines were, or what they were for. Except for one.

When the daughters were sick, I sometimes saw them take what I now know was DayQuil. I knew where that medicine was on the shelf and knew what it looked like. It came in tiny packets, maybe ten to a box. If I took one, would The Mom notice that one of the packets was missing? I was terrified but knew I had to take the risk.

I waited until The Mom was busy somewhere else in the house before I went to clean her bathroom. Then I quickly, cautiously took a packet out of the DayQuil box, quietly closed the cabinet door, and went into the bathroom in the upstairs hall. There, with trembling fingers, I opened the packet, swallowed the pill, and drank water directly from the sink to wash it down. Then I threw the packet into the trash and gathered the rest of the waste out of the can and brought it down to the big garbage bin in the garage. I didn't know if it was from fear or if it was from my illness, but my heart raced throughout the entire process.

The DayQuil did help some, but it was more than a week before I felt better. Now I understand that I have a weak immune system. This might be due to genetics, or it might be because I was not able to eat balanced meals when I was young. Or it might be that because I was overworked and underfed, my body has never been able to right itself. Whatever the cause, every year in May or June, I regularly come down with a bad cold. My throat swells and I become ill enough that I am often hospitalized.

Today I am grateful for health care, for the medical professionals who treat me, and for my friends who care for me and support me, because I know too well what it is like not to have that. It is easy to take these things for granted, but I never do. Ever.

As they had in Egypt, the days here in the United States wore on—and on. Birthdays and holidays came and went. The school year started and ended. I had stopped thinking about a future away from The Mom and The Dad and their entitled children. I only wanted to get through the next minute, the next hour, the next day. Some people might have turned to religion for comfort, but even that was denied me.

When I lived with my mom and dad when I was young, we were not heavily into religion. We were Muslim—as were most of the people in our town—but we went to the mosque only on days of celebration, even though my mom prayed what seemed like all the time. My captors, however, made many empty gestures toward practicing their Muslim faith.

My captor family regularly went to the mosque to pray. I did think a lot about the fact that this family acted religious, quoted the prophet Muhammad at the drop of a hat, and read the Koran every day, yet never did a good turn and were disrespectful to others. Never once were they kind to others. Even now it amazes me that they treated people like crap, yet they prayed with their prayer beads several times a day. My thought was that obviously the prayer beads were not working.

The family's behavior during the holy month of Ramadan was a good example of how they were. Ramadan is observed during the ninth month of the Islamic calendar year, and among other things, observers are supposed to fast every day from dawn to sunset. Observers are supposed to abstain from eating, drinking, smoking, and swearing during daylight hours, but I never saw much evidence of this with The Mom or The Dad or their family. Yes, there was less food and they went to the mosque more often, but that was about it. They were still the same entitled, demanding people.

Even though religion was not a huge part of my young childhood, I found familiarity and comfort in it and was sad that my captors did not allow me to participate in any of their religious

traditions. I was never allowed to go to the mosque when I was
with this family.

If I had not been utterly exhausted at the end of the day, I
might have tried to keep up with some of my own religious traditions. But I was always mentally and physically drained to the
point where I couldn't find the strength to even think about it.
One day, though, my Muslim faith was unexpectedly brought to
the forefront. That day was to become forever ingrained in people's
minds as 9/11.

I was in the kitchen that morning when the oldest daughter in
the house cried out, "Oh my God!" as she stared at the TV. There
was a lot of yelling and screaming after that, enough to bring The
Mom and The Dad downstairs from their bedroom. They were
watching the horrific events unfold on an Arabic news channel,
and I was able to pick up some of what was going on, although I
didn't understand much of it. I understood the Arabic words but
not the context in which they were said.

This was the first time I had seen my captor family shaken.
They were unnerved by what the terrorists had done, and they
soon became frightened. Right after 9/11 it seemed as if all
Americans were leery of anyone who looked as if they might
be from the Middle East. Even though the United States was
founded on the principle of freedom of religion, it was not a
good time to be Muslim.

The family mainly stayed in the house in the days and weeks
following the attack. When The Mom went out for groceries, as

she eventually had to do, she took off her head scarf. This was the first time she had ever done this in public. She didn't allow her hair to be completely uncovered, though. She wore a hat. There are many Hispanic people in Southern California, and I think The Mom tried to blend in with that population.

The oldest daughter refused to remove her head scarf, and there were huge fights between her and The Mom about that. It became an ongoing thing for them to argue violently about, but as the immediacy of 9/11 passed, the amount and intensity of the disagreements eventually lessened.

I found it interesting, though, that my captors did not seem to have any sympathy for the thousands of 9/11 victims or their families. Rather, they were afraid something bad might happen to them. I had to remind myself that we were in the United States in the first place because The Dad had gotten into some bad trouble in Egypt and it was safer for him and his family to leave Egypt. Now the family was afraid they might be deported. They were so afraid to leave the house, in fact, that they stopped going to the mosque. For a religious family such as this to be that fearful, I knew the situation was serious.

As for me, when it finally dawned on me what had happened, I couldn't believe it. How can anyone of any faith be heartless enough to kill so many people? It was beyond my comprehension then, and still is. Although I had issues with a lot of the Muslim culture, I knew that being Muslim was not about destruction but about loving and serving God. These monsters who changed the course of history are not representative of the vast majority who follow the Muslim faith. Since then I have learned that there are small groups of extremists in many faiths.

One of the problems I had with the Muslim faith and Arab culture in general was that they are both patriarchal, meaning that the man of the house rules. Many men, including most of the Muslim men I had come into contact with thus far, interpreted that as ruling with an iron fist. These men were quick to anger, and the result of their anger was verbal and physical abuse directed at whoever was in their path.

I didn't realize it then, but my early years, and then my time with my captors, had turned me into an emotionally strong person. The heavy responsibility of caring for my siblings at an early age had made me capable of taking care of myself, and I had developed an odd sort of street smarts. That's why, as time went on, I began to see these angry Arab men more as cartoon characters who were full of themselves, rather than people worthy of respect. These men were dangerous cartoon characters, though, and I took as much care as I could to stay away from any Arab man.

I didn't have any concept of other religions then, other than that back home in Egypt I knew there were Jewish people. My parents felt, however, that those of the Muslim faith should not associate with them, and that sentiment was echoed throughout our neighborhood. After my long, long days, when I finally lay in my bed in the cramped, stuffy room in the garage, I prayed to a God of all religions. Every night I prayed, "Please let me go home.

I hate the way people treat me here. I miss my family. Please let me go home."

Most nights I fell asleep saying those words over and over in my head. As the days, weeks, and months passed, I began to believe that God didn't love me, because nothing in my world changed. I wasn't sent home, and the family treated me in the same crappy way they always had. The Mom was the worst. She was brutal. While the entire family knew I was there to take care of anything they wanted, The Mom most of all knew how to use that power against me. She made me feel like a nobody, and I was too young and uneducated to have the skills to overcome that negative kind of thinking. I hated each of them, but her most of all.

I began to think that I'd never be able to leave this family, never have a life of my own. I had not a single moment of happiness during this time. Not one. This resulted in my having no feeling, no emotion during the day, but my subconscious must have gotten overloaded, because most nights I had terrible nightmares.

One nightmare sticks in my mind because I have it to this day. In it I am in Egypt with my mom. We are in the middle of the street, and in the street there is a round metal manhole cover that leads to a sewer. In my dream my mom lifts the cover, puts me in the sewer, and then closes the lid. It is dark and damp around me, and I scream and scream. I am afraid, and I don't understand why my mom has done this to me.

In the weird way of dreams, while I am trapped inside the sewer, I can see outside of it too. I see my mom take a blanket that we had in our apartment—checked with white, light blue, and dark blue—and place it over the lid to the sewer. Invariably, when I wake up from that dream, I am crying.

Even though I would cry out during and after the nightmare, there was no one to hear me, to give me comfort. I'd wake with these horrible images in my mind, covered with sweat, my heart pounding. Then I'd sit there in the dark and hug myself as I cried.

It doesn't take a rocket scientist to see the correlations between my dream and my real life. In both scenarios my mother essentially threw me away and trapped me in a life I did not want to lead. The result was that I became terrified of going to sleep and I never slept well. That's something that continues to this day.

The memory of my family was the only thing that kept me going through these tough times, even though I was often filled with hate for my mom and dad. I thought they should have fought harder to keep me in Egypt. They should have tried to get me back from my captors. But they didn't. From their perspective what had happened to me was "unfortunate," but it was an accepted part of life.

I never understood what part of my life as a slave could be acceptable. Many times The Mom told me, "Look at all we are doing for you. You live in a nice house with a dry roof over your head, and we provide you with a happy environment. You are a lucky girl." I wished she could walk in my shoes for a day. Then maybe she wouldn't have said such ridiculous things.

While anger at my situation was slowly filling my being, fortunately, I didn't have too much time to dwell on it. I was too busy
being mistreated, getting up way too early, and being yelled at.
Because I was the only servant the family had now, if something
went wrong, there was no one other than me for them to blame.
It made me furious, and I wondered how I could contain all my
anger. But I did.

I believe that the only way I kept any dignity or sense of self
was during the few hours I had to myself in the middle of the
night. That was my time, and I could finally let down my guard
and be me. During the day I had to be subservient, keep my eyes
lowered, and smile—even though I was often seething inside. That
was not me. By nature I am a person who speaks her mind. I have
definite thoughts and opinions, and before I had gone to live with
my captors, I had regularly shared my feelings with the people
around me.

Now, in the middle of the night, I thought mostly about my
younger brothers and sisters. I had managed to hold on to the
photo of my family that my mother had packed in my suitcase in
Egypt, and at night I often held it and brushed my fingers across
the faces of my younger siblings. Where were they now? What
were they doing? I hated that I was missing out on their lives.
Even though I had been in charge of them, that had been my
fun time, my "kid" time. With them I'd had the freedom to move
around our neighborhood, the freedom to play games, to make
choices. Now all of that was gone.

These nighttime hours were the only time I had to take care of *my* needs, bathing, washing my clothes, et cetera. I wasn't allowed to use the washer and dryer in the house. That was for the family's clothes. And besides, not too long after I had arrived, The Mom had said, "Stupid, your clothes are too dirty for our machines." That was why at night I washed my shirt, pants, and underwear in a bucket in the garage. Then I squeezed them out and hung them up to dry on a clothesline in the night darkness of the backyard.

When I outgrew my clothes, I was given hand-me-downs from one of the daughters. This worked okay until I was ten and began to develop. At first I didn't have a bra, but then someone must have noticed my changing body, and The Mom gave me an old bra that no longer fit her girls. It didn't fit me, either. It was way too tight and pinched me everywhere.

One day when I was ten I got my period. I was doing my chores when I felt a sharp pain and then some wetness. No one had ever spoken to me about the birds and the bees, but I had figured out a lot from the cleaning I did in the daughters' rooms. While I had expected my period to come at some point, I was not prepared for the excruciating pain that came with it. I had horrible bloating and cramps, but as with the flu, I was not allowed any kind of medication to relieve the symptoms.

As soon as The Mom got up, I looked at the floor and asked, "Ma'am, may I please have a pad?" I had heard the girls ask The Mom for pads when their periods came, and I figured I would be given some too. She did give me some, but these weren't the same pads that she and her girls used. My pads were a much cheaper brand that didn't hold up. Once, The Mom accused me of stealing her good pads. I hadn't, of course. I was far too frightened of her to do that. In the middle of her rant about how useless I was, I heard her say, "You don't deserve good pads."

Really? What had I done, other than be a good girl, to not deserve decent sanitary pads? I was beside myself with anger and began to ask God why my life was the way it was. I understood that many people in Egypt and in other parts of the world lived a life like mine. But I knew it was wrong and vowed that someday I would do what I could to change that. No one, not a single person, ever deserves to have their life, their freedom, stolen.

Here in the United States I was not allowed to answer the door. Anyone could be on the other side. But one day either a friend or a cousin of The Dad came to visit. He brought his family . . . and a girl like me, a slave. This family actually came several times, and over the course of the visits the girl told me she was planning to run away.

"I know where they keep my passport," she said.

I knew where my passport was kept too, but I dared not leave. The heavy threat of harm to my family weighed on me. Even though I was conflicted about my feelings for my parents and what they had allowed to happen to me, I didn't want any harm to come to them. I was especially concerned about my younger siblings.

Besides, where would I go? I didn't read any English and spoke only a word or two. Saying "hi" out on the street wouldn't bring me much safety or describe my plight to anyone. I had no knowledge of the culture here. I thought I might even be sent back to my captors. Then life would have been far worse than it was now. I thought I might be sent to a horrible prison where I would be beaten daily. No, I could not leave. Not now. Not ever.

CHAPTER SIX

*Even though I could not risk an escape attempt, oppor-*tunities did come about a few times. On several occasions my captors went on family trips, and when they did, they took me with them. Once they went camping at Big Bear Lake. Big Bear is a popular vacation spot in the San Bernardino National Forest about ninety miles northeast of Irvine, where we lived. Because there was no seat for me in the family's SUV, I rode in the tiny space behind the backseat, with the luggage. Well, with everyone else's luggage. I didn't have any, nor did I bring anything with me other than the shirt and pair of pants that I wore.

As you might imagine, it was quite cramped and uncomfortable back there. Plus, the ride seemed to take forever, and the summer sun beat down on me through the windows. Even though the SUV had air-conditioning, with the many bags and me packed into such a small space, there was little air circulation.

The way I sat on the floor of the vehicle, I was not visible to other drivers. Even if I had been seen through the vehicle's heavily tinted windows, I doubt that anyone would have called the police. It was illegal for me to be riding back there, but just as many states have laws that prohibit people from riding in the back of a moving pickup truck, it's not a law that is often enforced. Today I shudder to think what might have happened to me if we had gotten into an accident. If our SUV had been rear-ended, or if someone had hit the back panel near where I was sitting, I would not have stood much of a chance.

However, I could see out the windows. This was the first time I had ever seen mountains or woods, and I was greatly impressed, especially with the tall peaks. I think that's why this trip is clearly imprinted in my mind, because I was so impressed with the scenery. I had time to think during the drive, and I understood that the family was going on a vacation, but I didn't know where, or for how long. I had become accustomed to not knowing the bigger picture of things and had learned to let life's events unfold around me. What other choice did I have? There was nothing, absolutely nothing, in my life that I could control.

Eventually we pulled up to a huge cabin, and as the family's excitement grew, I unloaded the luggage and brought it inside. The kids ran from room to room while I struggled to match each suitcase with the right person and the right bed. The cabin was big, with two bedrooms: a room for The Mom and The Dad and the twins, and one for the girls. There was a bed for everyone—except me. I slept on the floor of the girls' room with only a blanket to cover me.

Friends of the family arrived later, and when everyone went out to explore during the ensuing days, I stayed in the cabin. Every day I sat on a chair in the kitchen. There was nothing to eat, nothing to watch, nothing to wash, fold, cook, or clean. I didn't want to fall asleep, because I knew The Dad would slap me if he came home to find me sleeping. Instead I sat, not knowing if they would come tumbling through the front door in an hour or later that evening.

When the family did come back, everyone wanted something at once, and I rushed to accommodate everyone. Once or twice, though, I got to walk in the woods with the twins, and I appreciated that experience. I loved the quiet, the peacefulness of the tall, tall trees, and I wished I could stay forever.

Another time the family went to Disneyland. Our house in Irvine was not far from there, but the drive to and from made it an extra long, busy day. My job while we were at the theme park was to watch the twins, give them their snacks when they were hungry, and wait with them in line for various rides. I didn't ride on anything, of course. I tried to become invisible. I was afraid that someone would ask why I was not going on the rides with the other kids, afraid they'd ask where my parents were. I was about eleven by this time, but I was small and looked much younger. And while the boys had been fluent in English even back in Egypt, I still didn't read, speak, or understand it.

The boys were excited to be at Disneyland, but I didn't know what to think about it. There was nothing like it back home in Egypt—at least that I had been aware of. In truth I thought Disneyland was weird. Everyone acted silly there, and I didn't understand the purpose of it. I held the boys' backpacks and waited. For me, Disneyland was just another place. You'd think I would have had some interest in the activities that were going on, but it says a lot about my state of mind and how much my captors had beaten down my spirit that I didn't.

While Disneyland didn't stir up my interest, a trip to SeaWorld did. There I got to sit in the audience and watch the shows, and I adored every second of the entertainment. I loved the water, the animals, and the people. This was the first time that I had ever been to any kind of entertainment or show. I had never even been to a movie—or to a concert or a play. I think that's why I was enamored of SeaWorld. I hadn't realized anything like that could exist.

I was so engaged at SeaWorld, in fact, that I even learned a new word, "dolphin." In addition to the fabulous shows, there was a section of the park where you could pay a fee to swim with the dolphins, and the girls signed right up. They disappeared into a small building, only to reappear a few minutes later in underwater suits. Then they went into one of the tanks and swam with the dolphins. My job was to videotape them while they were in the water. I had never used a video camera before, but The Dad turned it on and handed it to me. I then looked through the viewfinder and recorded the girls having a ton of fun.

Years later this video became one of the videos that was used in the legal case against my captors. While I was not seen on camera, my voice could be heard, and the video and audio clearly showed that I was not "part of the family." My captors told authorities that I was.

Either The Mom or The Dad taped other events from that day too. In one shot I was sitting next to their kids, and I laughed along with them at the antics going on in the pool. My captors used that one single instance of me being a normal kid to try to persuade the United States government that the family had treated me well. Thank goodness authorities could see my captors for who and what they were.

The Mom and The Dad did not seem worried about my being out in public during these special family days. After all, I knew only three words: "hi," "dolphin," and "stepsister." I didn't even know the meaning of the last word. I had been taught how to say it in case anyone ever asked about me. What trouble, my captors must have thought, could I bring upon myself with those three words?

One of the many rules in my captors' house was that only Arabic was spoken. I do not know if that was so the kids would have more of their own culture around them, if it was because The Mom and The Dad felt as if this little jaunt to the United States was going to be short and they'd soon head back to Egypt, or if it was to keep me from learning any English. In any case, I understood the twins well one day when they said in Arabic, "Mom, that stupid girl is being mean to us." The result was that she slapped me hard across my face. This was one of several times when The Mom slapped me. Usually it was The Dad.

In this instance, though, my tone had been somewhat sharp with the twins, out of frustration. It was in the evening. I had gotten their toothbrushes out and had put the toothpaste on, as I always did, but when I said, "Boys, it's time to brush your teeth," they ignored me. One of my many responsibilities was to keep the twins on a schedule. Bedtime was at eight thirty every evening, and I knew The Mom and The Dad would be unhappy with me if the boys did not get to bed on time.

"Boys," I said again. "Bedtime. Time to stop watching television and brush your teeth." The third time I repeated the request, they told The Mom I was mean to them.

The slap hurt. The first thought that went through my head, however, was that I should have yelled at the boys as loud as I could. If I was going to get slapped that hard for trying to do my job, then the slap for letting my temper loose on the boys couldn't have been that much harder.

Another time The Mom accused me of doing something with regard to the boys that I hadn't done. When I tried to explain, she called me a liar, grabbed me by the shoulder, and pushed me. Hard. Slapping, pushing, and screaming were part of life in that house. Both The Mom and The Dad yelled at me constantly.

Whenever I didn't get something done fast enough, or thoroughly enough, I'd hear, "This is your job! Who else gets up to do your job? This is not my job. It is your job, stupid girl!" This would usually be followed by a stream of derogatory words, such as, "You're nothing, nobody. You're stupid. You're lucky to be here. No one else would want you."

The Mom was a master at making many of the people around her feel like dirt. In fact, she addressed me in a yelling tone of voice more often than she spoke to me. Her kids were spared her temper, but they were often on the receiving end of The Dad's anger. In fact, I was far more afraid of him than I was of her. Every day The Mom told him how unhappy she was with me, what a bad attitude I had. I tried to avoid him, but it wasn't always possible. When she yelled, I could stand there and take it. When he yelled, I flinched and cowered. I couldn't help it. My fear of him was that great. Once he slapped me so hard that my face tingled for days.

As the months wore on, I lost track of time. I had no idea how long I had been there, or even how old I was. I couldn't even remember what day I was born. Certainly none of my birthdays were celebrated, although one day a daughter was a bit less hateful to me and told me it was because it was my birthday.

The oldest daughter eventually graduated from high school and began going to college, although she still lived at home. The middle daughter was well into her high school years, and the younger girl, the girl who was my age, was in middle school. The twins were finishing up elementary school.

In all those years I never saw a doctor or a dentist. I never went to a grocery store, a restaurant, or to the library. In fact, I always thought that every single thing that was purchased came from the same place. I thought there was a big store that had everything, like Walmart, but I never considered that there were other stores too.

I had no idea how long I had been held in bondage, but I had lost any hope that anything in my life would change. I was resigned to the fact that I would grow old with this family and in my lowly position in the home.

There were many moments when I hated God, even though I prayed every day. Who else was there for me to talk to? There were many times when I was angry, when I missed my family badly enough that I couldn't sleep. Some days I wanted to kick and scream at my captors. I wanted to slap them across the face, like they slapped me. But I never did. I was too afraid.

In the back of my mind I knew that holding another person captive, as I was being held, was wrong. I knew that every family did not have someone like me who slept in the garage. Even though I couldn't see how, or when, I hoped that someday I would be free of this family and my life could get better. I hoped with all I had that I would be able to see my younger brothers and sisters again. I recalled bits and pieces of them, and the place where we'd lived. Some nights I'd even dream of getting into a taxi that would carry me across the United States and the ocean, and back to our crowded two-room apartment in Egypt.

That never happened, never could happen. But something else

did. Someone—a neighbor maybe, or a mom who had seen me at the park, or possibly someone who had seen me with the boys at the pool—someone, a wonderful someone, made a phone call.

This unknown person might have spotted me at midnight when I was hanging the clothes out to dry, or through the kitchen window at two in the morning when I was still washing dishes. However he or she learned about me, they questioned how I was being treated and did the right thing. They made a call. That call ended up in the hands of both the local office of Child Protective Services and the local police department. The local office of US Immigration and Customs Enforcement was also called. These are the people who deal with the realities of human trafficking, who rescue people like me. And they did.

CHAPTER SEVEN

The morning of April 9, 2002, dawned like any other. It was a Tuesday, a school day, and The Mom and The Dad, along with the oldest daughter, were upstairs. As I always did, I had risen early to get the twins and the two younger daughters off to school.

I was downstairs when there was a knock on the door. It was a loud knock, the kind that you hear on television during a police show. I was not allowed to answer either the phone or the door, so I ignored the sound. But then the knock came again and it was loud enough to bring The Dad down the stairs. I had already served him and The Mom their morning coffee, and knew he was awake. He looked surprised as he rumbled down the stairs, and then he peeked through the peephole in the front door. Then he told me to go into his office. I went. I needed to clean that room anyway.

When he opened the door, there was a lot of yelling. It was in

English, so I didn't understand the words, but I did understand that The Dad was angry. The ruckus was enough to bring the older daughter out to the balcony that overlooked the foyer. The Mom was there too, except she stayed out of sight near the top of the stairs the entire time.

I was done in the office and was on my way to the kitchen, but I had to briefly go through the hall to get there. The Dad had told me to stay in the office, but I had a lot of work to do. If I got too far behind, then The Mom would yell at me. Like a lot of situations in that house, this was a no-win for me. No matter what I did, someone would be mad. I hoped I could avoid being slapped. I was more afraid of The Dad than The Mom, so I went back into the office.

Eventually I heard the door slam, and The Dad said in Arabic, "I didn't have to let them in. They didn't have a warrant."

I didn't yet understand that the authorities had come for me. The Dad had gotten into trouble in Egypt, and I thought it was more of that. Specifically what "that" was, I didn't know. But I knew The Mom and The Dad thought it was bad. The Mom and The Dad talked for a few minutes. Then there was another loud knock on the door. Plus, this time the doorbell rang. I'll never know why The Dad answered the door. He must have known who it was on the other side. He must have known they had gotten a warrant.

This time the officers were allowed into the house, and they were a lot madder than they'd been the first time. There was a lot more arguing and yelling, and then I was called to the door where a man physically put himself between The Dad and me. Then a woman took me by the hand and led me out of the house.

Before I was hustled out of the house, the Dad hissed into my ear, "Do not tell them anything. Say you do not work for me." I was terrified. For many years my captors had told me stories about all of the bad things that would happen to me if the police ever found me. Now those stories were at the forefront of my mind. My life with The Mom and The Dad had been awful, but I had been told that life with the police would be much, much worse. I did what The Dad said.

"I do not work here," I said in Arabic. "I do not work here."

The woman was nice and tried to talk with me, but she did not understand Arabic. My English of words "hi," "dolphin," and "stepsister" wouldn't go far here.

Before I knew it, I found myself in the front seat of a marked police car with a police officer. He handed me a phone, and I found a man who spoke Arabic on the other end. He was a translator, a person who knows two languages who helps people communicate with each other. This was exceptionally scary for me, and I wanted to cry. On top of my deep fear of authorities, everything in my Muslim culture forbade me to speak to a man who was not a member of my household. Plus, I had rarely spoken on the phone, as I had been forbidden to do so. Here I was breaking three taboos at once.

The man on the phone tried to reassure me that the people who had taken me out of my captors' home were not bad people. "These are good people, people who are there to rescue you from your bondage," he said. I was quite confused. I didn't know who or what to believe. I had been brainwashed for years about many things in life, especially the roles of people. My distorted view of who men, women, slaves, and authority figures were—and how they should act—was hard for me to discount.

Eventually I did start to cry, and when I started, I couldn't stop. I never knew my body could produce that many tears. Many things were rushing through my brain, but most of all I was concerned about what would happen to me. My brain kept defaulting to what I had always been taught. Police were bad. If asked, I was to say I was a stepsister who was visiting.

Also, it had been a long time since anyone had treated me nicely and with respect, and I didn't know how to react when the officers were kind to me. My captors' home had been filled with fear, abuse, hatred—and constant physical, mental, and emotional battles. I could barely remember what a warm, loving, safe, nurturing environment was like.

After a while I settled down enough to tell the man on the phone my name. Then he asked what my dad's name was, and I told him. He asked a few other questions, such as if I had ever been to school and how long I had been in the country. The first question was easy. No, I had never been to school. Not here in the United States and not back home in Egypt. How long I had been in the US was another story, though. I didn't know. I later was startled to find that when I was rescued, I was six months shy of my thirteenth birthday. I had been in the United States for a little more than twenty months. It had seemed like forever.

I was taken by car from my captors' house in the gated community in Irvine, California, to what was then called Orangewood Children's Home. It has since been renamed the Orangewood Children and Family Center, but its services are basically the same. It is an emergency shelter for neglected and sexually, physically, or emotionally abused children, and is located in Santa Ana, California. Each year the home provides refuge for more than a thousand kids who have been removed from their caretakers and placed into protective custody.

It seemed like the ride took forever, although we couldn't have traveled much more than fifteen miles. Then again, in California traffic fifteen miles *can* take forever. I had no idea where I was going or what was happening. I didn't even understand that I had been rescued, that I would no longer have to serve The Mom and The Dad eighteen to twenty hours a day, or live in fear that he or she would slap me, or that their kids would yell at me. Instead, in the police car, I was so afraid of what might happen next that I shook throughout the entire ride.

When we arrived at Orangewood, I was first taken to the medical clinic, where I went through all sorts of tests. Then I was given a shot, and my hand, which had been hurting badly for a long time, was bandaged. Later a social worker named Hana Hana, a short, dark-haired

Arab woman with a kind face, told me it was broken, although I have no remembrance of what could have caused that to happen.

By this time the kindness everyone had shown me allowed me to relax some. There was no rudeness from anyone, no accusations, and no hitting or slapping. Even though I could not understand the words, I was able to understand the tone of voice, and that made me give them the tiniest bit of my trust.

Someone then took me to the housing area and showed me around the facility and to my room. After that I was directed to a large bathroom that was used by everyone on the floor. I took a shower and couldn't believe it when someone gave me a pair of pajamas. In all my life I had never worn pajamas. These pajamas had a black, gray, and white check pattern. They were so fresh and clean I couldn't believe I would be allowed to wear them. Compared to the dirty castoffs that I usually wore to sleep in, these clothes were amazing. I treasured the pajamas then and now, and the fact that I still have them shows how much they mean to me.

My long hair was apparently matted, and another kind lady brushed it for me. I didn't know when anyone had treated me as nicely, and here I was in a place where many people were wonderful. By this time I was overwhelmed and didn't know what to think. I was still crying and could not begin to process what was happening. I didn't understand that I was to stay there, didn't realize I was never to go back to the home of my captors. It was too much, and I was grateful when someone told me I could take a nap.

Later that day I was taken to a small conference room and

spoke in Arabic with Hana Hana, who explained to me that the people at Orangewood were nice people. "These people," she said, "don't like to see kids mistreated or taken advantage of. Instead they try to put kids in foster care with nice families or, even better, reunite the kids with their own families."

Hearing her words, I had my first glimmer of hope. Would I get to go home and see my family? Would I finally be able to hug my younger brothers and sisters and see my mom? All the anger I had toward my parents for allowing me to be mistreated by my captors melted away. Maybe my prayers were finally being answered.

After my conversation with Hana, a small group of people came into the room. Hana translated my words as a man asked questions such as:

"Shyima, who lives in The Mom and The Dad's house?"

I remained silent, and he tried again.

"What was your role there? What did you do?"

I was afraid to say anything, so I kept my mouth shut.

"What were your days like, Shyima? How did they treat you?"

I realized that the man was not going to give up. I had to say something. My captors had ingrained in me what I should say and do if a situation like this ever occurred, and I stayed close to their script. Even though I knew on some level that this was my chance to go home, I did what The Dad had told me to do and said, "Nothing was wrong in the house. The Mom and The Dad treated me like a daughter. Everything is fine." That's how terrified I still was of my captors.

The next day everyone came back and got my mom and dad on the phone. I couldn't believe I was going to get to talk with them. I had missed them badly and could not wait to talk to them! But my excitement was not to last long. When a different social worker told my dad what was going on, my dad began to yell at me as she listened on another extension in the room.

"How could you leave those people who took such good care of you?" he shouted. "Those people treated you right. How can you listen to these people now? By leaving the home of these people, you have disrespected me. And you have caused your mother to have a heart attack. You must go back and behave yourself."

As angry as he had often been when I was young, as angry as I had seen The Mom and The Dad, I had never heard such a hateful tone coming from another human being. My eyes welled, and tears soon streamed down my face. How could my dad say those things? How could he want me to go back to my captors, to live such a terrible life?

In the years since, I have been able to come up with only two answers to my questions of that day. One is money. I had been sold to my captors for a sum that was less than twenty dollars a month. Even though some of the money had gone to repay what my sister had stolen, I believe my parents were still getting part of it. Twenty dollars goes much further for a poor family in Egypt than it does here. Even so, it was not a huge sum.

The other reason is honor. My sister had disgraced our family, and it was my job to uphold honor for my mom and dad, and for my siblings. That may be hard for people here in the United States to understand, but in many other countries this is an important matter.

In the middle of my dad yelling at me, I found some nerve and began to yell back. "How dare you speak to me like this! How dare you suggest that I go back to a family that refused to provide me medical care, who regularly yelled at and slapped me, and made me sleep in a garage while they were surrounded by luxury. How dare you!"

It felt great to let loose and tell my father what I had been feeling. I had never yelled at him before. Even though I had been outspoken when I'd lived with my family, never had I been disrespectful enough to yell at either of my parents. In fact, once I got going, I didn't stop yelling for several minutes. That was about the maddest that I have ever been.

I then spoke to my mother. Briefly. I never learned if she had had a heart attack or not, or if I had been the cause of it. But she, in softer words and tone, echoed my dad. I couldn't believe that she, too, wanted me to stay. What had I ever done to deserve this? Back on the line my dad told the social worker that he was coming to get me, but she said, "No, you have no visa. You cannot come."

The reality was that after hearing my dad's rant, no one in the room, including me, had any assurance that my dad would not send me back into slavery. That's why I decided in that single moment that, no, I was not going to go back to Egypt. I was done with my parents. All my hopes and dreams of being reunited with my family had just been shattered. I, too, had been shattered, but I was not going to go back to Egypt or to my captors' house. No, I would take my chances with the foster care system here in the United States.

After the call ended, the translator wanted to talk with me, but my mind was spinning all over the place, and I refused. Instead I walked back to my room and stayed there by myself for the rest of the day.

Later that week I told the police about the slave girl who had visited us with her captors. In case she had not been able to run away, I wanted authorities to know about her. I was shown pictures of people that The Dad might have known, and I was able to pick out her captor. Sometime after that I learned that the police tried to find her, but by the time they got to the home, her family had left the country. In fact, they had probably fled within hours of learning of my rescue. That girl was older than I was, and she was smart. I think of her often and hope that she, too, found freedom.

It turned out that Orangewood was a good place. It was not as plush as either of my captors' homes, but it was by far the nicest place I had lived as a free person. The main part, where I lived, looked like a big house. When you walked in, there was a medical area on the left, and on the right was an area where parents could meet with their kids. I was to learn that many of the kids at Orangewood had been taken out of their parents' care for one reason or another. But as the family worked through their issues, the kids were often reunited with their mom and dad. Other kids went in and out of foster care and stayed at Orangewood between placements with foster families.

The house I was in had only girls. Inside there was a hangout area for us, game area, kitchen, and dining room. Outside there was a nice yard and a pool. I shared a room with a girl I'll call Autumn, who was about my age. She was as blond as I was dark, but she was friendly and caring, and she tried to calm me down whenever I got upset or overwhelmed—which, at first, was often. Because I didn't speak English, I didn't understand her words, but I could read her body language well. She became my first real friend.

I liked the comfort of our tiny room. Autumn and I shared a closet, and there were two beds, one for each of us on opposite sides of the room. And I have to say that the mattress on my bed was the most comfortable that I had ever slept on. I loved the bed-spreads, which were white with tiny flowers on them. The room had a big window so we could see outside, and the door to the hallway had a little window that staff could peek in to be sure we were okay.

While I was at Orangewood, I met kids from every kind of situation imaginable. I met bratty kids, kids with entitlement issues, kids who had been horribly abused, kids who were full of rage or sadness. I even met a ten-year-old who was pregnant. Being with that many different kinds of kids made me understand that while bad things can happen, there are a lot of people out there trying to do good. I hope if someone is going through a bad time, if they are being abused in any way, that they will find a teacher, boss, friend, social worker, counselor, or pastor—someone who will help get them out of that situation. The many different situations the kids came from, contrasted with the kind, helpful people at Orangewood, convinced me that there are many good people in this world.

Even though I was surrounded by kind people, I cried all the time. The horror of the trauma, of the abuse, and of missing my family, combined with my dad's betrayal, came pouring out in my tears. Slowly, as the days passed, I realized that I would get to stay at Orangewood, at least for a while. The relief that knowledge brought caused even more tears to fall. My years in captivity had taken a huge emotional toll.

One thing that helped me a lot was the regular routine at Orangewood. I'd had a routine in my captors' house, but this was different. When I had breakfast at Orangewood, I did not have to cook the food—for me or for anyone else. When it was time to go to bed, I had a real bed with real blankets and lots of time to sleep and recharge for the next day.

In my first weeks at Orangewood I regularly met with Hana and other social workers and law enforcement officials. One of these people was Mark Abend. Mark's job title is supervisory special agent, Homeland Security Investigations, Immigration and Customs Enforcement. He is what is known as an ICE agent. Mark told me that I was taken from the home of The Mom and The Dad because someone had seen me and thought something was not quite right. I was never in school and I worked all the time. I think the person who made the call might have been a neighbor who had seen me through a kitchen window when I was washing dishes late at night, but I will never know for sure. I am forever grateful that he or she called the local police.

Mark said, "After the police knocked on the door the first time and were denied entry, they got a warrant and came back. They asked your captor who lived in the house, and he named every person—except for you. When an officer pointed you out and asked why you were not in school, he replied that you did not want to go.

"When the officers finally entered the house," Mark continued, "they found your passport and saw that you had overstayed your three-month visitor's visa by about eighteen months. Those were the grounds on which you were removed from the home."

Sitting there at Orangewood with Mark, I tried to relax, but I couldn't. Mark used humor to try to get me to open up, but Arabic prohibition against male-female interactions stopped me from engaging with him. I could not understand his words without a translator, but his friendly vibe and his facial expressions almost made me smile. Almost.

While I appreciated Mark's efforts, I had other things to think about. School. My biggest challenge at Orangewood, by far, was school. I had never been inside a classroom, so the mechanics of school were foreign to me. What was toughest for me was that I didn't understand anything that was being said. Physically my butt was in the chair, but mentally I quickly learned to zone out. Imagine not knowing your letters or numbers, then being put into a middle school classroom in a country that not only doesn't speak your language but also doesn't use the same alphabet—China for instance. It was impossible for me to learn in that setting.

All was not lost, however. Hana Hana met with me many times, and I learned to trust her and over time came to consider her a friend. In addition to the Arabic words she spoke, she looked and acted as if she cared, and I appreciated her efforts on my behalf. Hana had my back and did her best to make Orangewood the best experience it could be for me. Hana helped Orangewood put special teachers and aides next to me in the classroom, and these people taught me letters, colors, and numbers. And slowly, very slowly, I began to pick up on some of it.

Hana explained that here in the United States everyone has rights and that all kids go to school. Through her I learned how mistreated I had been, and I made up my mind that no matter what else happened, I would never allow someone to mistreat me ever again. I was no longer a helpless, naïve, eight-year-old child. By now I was almost thirteen and had been around more than my share of abusive people. No more. No matter what else happened to me in the future, I was done with that. I was old enough to advocate for myself, to speak up and tell people what I needed. My social worker taught me that here in the United States people can make their own decisions. That alone was life changing for me.

Another issue was that, according to Hana and my team of other social workers and the staff at Orangewood, I should have been with my parents. But my mom and dad were in another country. If I were sent back to them, there was no guarantee that they would not sell me into slavery again. Hana and my team would not allow that to happen. It was an odd feeling for me to think that there were people who were watching out for me. That had been a rare occurrence in my life thus far.

I had told Hana about my brothers' touching my private parts and how icky that had made me feel. She made me see how wrong and unacceptable that was. Those two factors eventually kept me here in the United States. Even though my three-month visa had long since expired, and even though that visa had been obtained illegally, a wonderful woman judge in Orange County, California, felt I would not be safe if I were sent back to Egypt.

Several times Hana and I made the five-minute walk from Orangewood to the juvenile courthouse where various aspects of my case were heard. Several other social workers acted on my behalf too. On one visit the judge gave me a stuffed tiger. It was not the first such gift I received, as a woman at Orangewood had given me a little bear with a heart on it. This gift was especially important to me, though, because tigers are strong and stand up for themselves. To me that tiger meant hope. That tiny stuffed toy represented a better future. I still have it because the gift and what it stood for meant something to me then. And you know what? It still does.

CHAPTER EIGHT

I was at Orangewood for quite a few months before I was placed in a foster home. That was probably a good thing, because it took me a while to get used to doing everyday tasks that most people enjoy. Showering daily was one thing. And having shampoo, conditioner, toothpaste, soap, and other supplies was hard to get used to at first. Most people take these things and others, such as sleeping with a window and a light in the room, for granted, but I didn't. I still don't. When it came time to find placement for me, it was more difficult than for many of the other kids because I did not speak English. Plus, I was still way behind in my education. I was thirteen but was probably at a kindergarten level in school.

The other reason placement was difficult was that Orangewood made a real effort to screen their families well. Rather than put kids with just about anyone, as I have learned some other facilities do, the staff at Orangewood tried hard to find a good fit for their kids. Part of this process allowed the kids to interview the prospective foster parents, and to have the final say on whether or not they wanted to join the new family.

When I initially met my first foster family, I felt in the back of my mind that I was supposed to accept them no matter what. My prospective foster mom and her kids came to Orangewood, and we met in the parent area. I did like them. And this family was a Muslim one that spoke both English and Arabic, which was great because they could provide me with a strong transitional home. I knew nothing of American life. I had never been to a store or a restaurant and didn't know such things as libraries or movie theaters existed.

This family said the right things, but I was still mistrustful of people I didn't know, and especially of Muslim men. The men in my life so far had not been good to me, as all of them had been angry, domineering, and belligerent. But I wanted a family. I very much wanted to belong, and when the staff at Orangewood asked if I wanted to give this family a try, I said, "Sure. Let's go for it."

My first foster family lived about a fifteen-minute drive from Orangewood. It was a nice, calm neighborhood, with lots of retired people. There were several bedrooms and one bath in our home, along with the usual kitchen and living room.

I was thrilled to find that I had my own room. In it was a set of bunk beds—one stacked on top of the other—a chair, and a closet with no door. It was a small room, but it was mine and I was grateful for it. Next to me was my foster mom and dad's room, and behind that, another bedroom. To get to that room you either had to walk through the mom and dad's room or go outside and into the room through the back door. It was an odd layout.

My new family included a dad, Ahmed, who was originally from the Middle East and a mom, Sarah, who was from here in the United States. I thought of them as another version of The Mom and The Dad. Sarah was an aggressive woman of average height and blond hair who had been raised Christian but had converted to the Muslim faith when she married. Ahmed was tall and thick, and something about him gave me the creeps. I never felt comfortable around him and was never able to establish any kind of a relationship.

The couple had a son who was in his twenties who was in and out of the home with his own daughter, who was two or three. The second child was in high school, and neither of these siblings practiced their Muslim faith, even though they had been raised in it.

Ahmed and Sarah also had a young girl, who was two or three. This girl slept in the back bedroom. In addition there was a baby who slept in a crib in her parents' room.

This family was nice to me and tried hard, but I never felt that I fit in. I had nothing in common with the other kids, and we weren't close enough in age to be going through the same life stages together. There was a baby, a toddler, a kid in high school, a young man in his twenties—and me. Even though I knew this was supposed to be a long-term placement, every day when I woke up, I'd think, *What's next for me?*

Instead of going to school, as I had hoped I would be able to do, I was homeschooled. The family did this for religious purposes, and even though I was disappointed about it at the time, it was good for me because I got more personal attention than I would have had in public school. Both Arabic and English were spoken in the home, and I believe Orangewood wanted me placed with this family so I could learn to speak, read, and write English. In that way, I was where I needed to be.

I was homeschooled along with another Muslim family, and that mom taught us. She was a good teacher, but I was frustrated. Orangewood had given me a start, but I was far behind everyone else. I cried in frustration almost every day as I struggled to learn to say the names of letters, colors, and numbers. Then I had to learn to put meaning behind the words. I might be able to say the word "walk," for example, but it took much longer for me to differentiate the word from the action.

Slowly, however, some of it came together. I went from learning letters to understanding how to put the letters together to make words. Remember, I didn't even know how to do this in my native Arabic language, so every thought, concept, and idea was new to me. After I could make a few words, I learned how to put them together to make a sentence. And as my English speaking improved, my writing, reading, and comprehension did too. I was still way behind, though. Imagine being a teenager and struggling through first-grade work. That was me.

Eventually my social workers thought I was ready for more

and asked my foster parents to put me in school. Because this family was a traditional Muslim one, they would consider only Muslim schools. The first school they approached, the school that was closest to where we lived, felt I was too old for the grades they offered. They were concerned that the age difference between their elementary school students and me would prove to be too much for both the other kids and me to overcome. They may have been right.

I did go for a brief time to another Muslim school, though. This school had kids my age, but even though the administrators put me into their special education classes, I was too far behind for their teachers to help me. I was perfectly happy to end up back in our little home school.

One reason I wanted to be there was that I liked my teacher a lot. She was kind and patient with me, as were her daughters, who were the other students. Of the two daughters, there was a girl my age and one a year younger. While both became dear friends, I spent more time with the younger daughter, Assana. It turned out that I wasn't just way behind in my formal education. I was far behind in my social skills too, and because Assana was younger, she was closer to me on that level.

Without the opportunity to form friendships and play, as most other kids do, I had missed out on important developmental milestones. The preteen birthday parties, young-girl crushes on the boy next door, sleepovers, Girl Scouts, choir practice, camping, sports—I had experienced none of the normal things that other young girls do in America. My teacher and her girls helped me experience several of those things for the first time, and I am pleased that I got to share those times with these wonderful people.

I loved Assana and her family and stayed overnight at their home often. There I learned to ride a bike and use a computer. On a social level I didn't understand that there was work time, playtime, break time, homework time, et cetera, and they helped me over that little hump of understanding too.

At this point in time I was a quiet person. I was unsure of what to say or do when I was around other people. And if I had something to say, my English was often not good enough for me to express my feelings. Assana was also a quiet person, and we became the kind of friends who understand each other intuitively. I often watched her to see what she would say or do in a given situation, so just by being herself she was teaching me.

While I enjoyed my time with Assana and her family, life with my foster family wasn't turning out to be everything I had hoped. One reason was that I was overwhelmed with everything about my new life. I know I have used that word a lot, "overwhelmed," but I have no other word to describe how emotionally overloaded I was. It was still hard for me to believe that simple freedoms—such as being able to sleep later than daybreak on a weekend morning, or sitting down at a table to eat rather than serving the meal—were mine.

I had had such a rigid schedule with my captors, and there had also been a routine at Orangewood. I had hated the first and enjoyed the second, but with my foster family the schedule was less formal, and that meant I had more time to myself. That was another new concept for me: personal time. I had no idea what I should do when I wasn't responsible for something or someone else. There had never been time for me to explore my interests or talents, so I didn't even know what I liked to do. Hike, sing, draw, play cards—I had no clue what I was good at or how to spend my time.

I ended up spending most of my free time alone in my room. I did puzzles and played with flash cards, both of which I am sure helped me developmentally but weren't that exciting. My room became my best friend because there was a lot of arguing going on in my foster home. I'd had enough of that with my biological parents, and with The Mom and The Dad, and didn't want to get involved in the fighting in this home too.

Although Ahmed was a kinder person than the other men in my life, he still was the authority figure. None of us dared question his decisions—except his mother-in-law, Sarah's mother, who made it clear that she did not approve of Muslims.

The mother-in-law visited often. But whenever the arguing became too intense, she'd leave in a huff. Life always settled down when she was away, but after a few days, boom, there she was again.

For some reason this woman did not seem to like me and I did not feel welcome there. I don't know if she thought I was taking up a room that the baby could be in. Or maybe she thought *she* should have been sleeping in the room that I was in. It's possible that she just didn't like me. Whatever the reason, I think she went out of her way to get me in trouble.

"Shyima pinched the baby," she'd say. Of course I did no such thing, but she was always saying things like that.

To make life even more difficult, my foster dad and I did not get along well. There was no connection between us, and he always wanted me to go to the mosque with them. Some who practice the Muslim faith go to their place of worship every day, but most families, including this one, didn't. Instead they usually went weekly and on special days within the faith. The reason I didn't like to go was that it was the same mosque that The Mom and The Dad went to. They were still under investigation and had not been convicted of anything yet, which meant they were free to enjoy everything the United States had to offer, including this particular mosque. One time we went, and I saw The Mom there. I had such a horrible feeling when I saw her. I told my foster parents, and they agreed that I would not have to go back if I didn't want to. I went a few times after that but did not see her or any other members of her family there again. Even so, that mosque remained an uneasy place for me to be.

When I had been with my captors in Egypt, I had spoken with my biological mother once or twice. Now my social workers and my foster dad encouraged me to speak to my parents again, even though it had been a while since we had talked. My social worker thought it was important that we keep the lines of communication open, so my foster dad made the calls even though I didn't want to. I knew the outcome would be the same as it had been when we'd spoken when I was in Egypt, and when we'd spoken just after I had been rescued. I was right.

The first time I talked to my dad when I was with this foster family, all he did was yell at me. "Your mother is very sick, and it is all your fault," he said. Forget the fact that she had eleven children and little in the way of medical care or good food. When he said, "You are a selfish child to be in that place you are now," I began to cry, and the tears only became larger when he said, "You should be here, home with your family."

How could he even say that? For years I had wanted nothing more than to be home with my family. The reason I wasn't was because he and my mother had sold me into slavery. Now he dared to yell at me for not being there? I could think of nothing that was more unfair than his treatment of me.

Even though there was a chance I would be sold back into slavery, even though my brothers had touched me inappropriately, if either my dad or my mom had said in a kind tone, "We love you, we miss you, we are sorry for what happened. We can't wait for you to come home, where we can give you a hug," I might have thought about asking my social worker to make that happen.

The reality was, in an ideal world I did want to be with my biological family. I desperately wanted to catch up on the lost years, and I missed my younger brothers and sisters a lot. But I had learned that we do not live in a perfect world. Even though life was tough for me now, it was significantly better than it had been before. I knew I was where I needed to be.

My foster dad saw how much the phone call upset me, so several months later when my social worker thought we should try again, he was on the line with me. He interrupted my dad's rants several times, and even became angry when my dad again blamed my mother's heart attack on me. Even though we didn't get along, I was glad that my foster dad defended me.

The third and last time I spoke with my parents during this period in my life, I got to talk to my mom and several of my brothers and sisters. My heart melted when my mother said, "I miss you more than I can say." Then it hardened right back up when my dad got on the line and said, "Whenever I see you, I will march right up to you and kick you." When my dad went on to say, "I am going to the president of the United States to tell him that the United States has stolen my daughter," my foster dad once again intervened.

By this time my foster parents and my social workers could see that these calls were not the least bit helpful, and in fact only made matters worse. I was thankful when I learned I would not have to make those calls to Egypt anymore.

About this time I began to see an Arabic therapist. I didn't talk much but I listened far more than my body language said I did.

I was prescribed medication for anxiety and depression. This was in addition to medication I had been prescribed at Orangewood for insomnia. I think it helped, for a while. One thing was for sure: Family life was a lot more complicated than I had thought it would be.

In my foster home I was allowed to wear whatever I wanted inside the home, including makeup, which I love to this day. I had no allowance, but I had done enough good deeds at Orangewood that I had earned enough tokens to pick out a gift, and I had chosen a young girl's makeup kit, which I treasured.

Whenever I went out, though, I had to cover my head with the hijab, even though I didn't agree with it. To my foster dad, wearing the hijab was a sign of a woman's respect for herself. I did not agree with any man who told a woman how to best respect herself. I didn't yet know that the United States was a country of religious freedom—that I could worship and pray to God in any manner that I chose. All I knew was that I did not believe in any religion that made women into second-class citizens, and where the man of the house could berate everyone around him.

I have since learned that not every Muslim home is like this, and that is not what the Muslim faith is about. But from my experience and perspective at the time, that's what I felt it was. I respect people of all faiths, and respect their religious beliefs. I fully honored my friend Assana's decision to wear the hijab. I didn't want to be Muslim, though, and that caused a lot of stress between my foster family and me.

Another thing that was not working with this placement was that my foster mom continually corrected my English, and not in a positive manner. Rather than say, for example, "Shyima, that was better. But next time try saying 'you' with an 'ooo' sound instead of an 'aw' sound," instead Sarah would say, "You didn't say it right. How many times do I have to tell you?" Once, Sarah's snide tone and harsh words were so evident that even her older son defended me.

Sarah's attitude made me shut down emotionally toward her. One thing I have learned about myself is that when people do not understand that I am trying my hardest, I disconnect from them. If they cannot recognize the effort I am making, even though I do not always get things right, I don't want to have anything more to do with that person.

Basically Sarah was nice, but she had listened too much and too long to her own mother. Day after day both women made my life difficult. Nothing I did was right. Some of the fighting that started between us, though, was my beginning to assert my own individuality and opinions. Looking back, this was a huge milestone. I was displaying normal teen defiance! But once, after a particularly heated argument, Sarah's mother said, "That's it. It's either Shyima or me."

I didn't leave right away. With the help of my social worker, we looked around for a new foster family while I remained in my current home. I spent a few nights with different families, but none was a good fit until an opportunity in Arizona came along. Sarah even went with me to visit this new family over a long weekend. My English was much improved, but I was still far behind other kids my age in every possible way, and I knew that any placement was going to be difficult. But I wanted to show everyone that I had a positive attitude and was doing my part, so I agreed to stay with this new family. Unfortunately, we could all see right away that the fit was not good, and when the school in Arizona said they didn't know what to do with me, I came back.

I learned a lot from my first foster family. I had many firsts with them, and with Assana's family, and I felt that I was starting to fit into American life. I was with this family for nearly two years, and during my second year there I even began thinking some phrases in English. That was another huge milestone.

Through the years I saw many social workers. I believe they had to swap cases with others in their office every few months to prevent a social worker from getting too invested in someone like me and losing their objectivity. I also, on occasion, had conversations with Mark Abend through an interpreter. In my meetings with him I learned that the United States government was still investigating my former captors. I also knew there was a jurisdictional fight brewing over who was going to handle the case. For some reason the FBI wanted it, but Mark was adamant that his division of Homeland Security was going to prosecute. I didn't care.

It was far too much for me. I was busy trying to deal with daily life—trying to learn English and fit in with other kids my age—

and didn't want to be brought into the case. I had no desire to ever see my captors again and thought if they fell off the face of the earth, that would be fine with me.

I understood that building the case would take time, so I didn't think too much about it. My mind was directed instead toward my next foster family.

CHAPTER NINE

My second foster home turned out to be in central Cali-
fornia, and I was again living with a Muslim family. There was a
mom and a dad, Rachel and Manjit, and an older girl who was in
college but who lived at home. There was also a boy who was in
high school, and then a younger girl.

The landscape there was much greener and far more beautiful than I was used to. Many of the trees and shrubs were
different from those in Orange County, and it took some time
for me to get used to the change. Even though most of the city
was clean, we lived in a run-down area. But the home was larger
and nicer than I had lived in for my first foster placement, and
even had a pool.

Instead of having my own room, I shared with the family's older
daughter. I came to this family right after the first of the year, and
for the first time I was able to go to public school. The other kids

in the family went to a Muslim school, but as had happened with my first foster placement, I was far enough behind for my age that the Muslim school here was not equipped to educate me. In public school I was put in the eighth grade even though my education level was in the lower elementary grades. I believe that my social workers had recommended that I be with kids closer to my own age because I was quite far behind socially.

I was excited about school. My English was good enough that I could make my needs known, and if people spoke slowly, I understood a lot of what they said. I was looking forward to making friends and learning as much as possible so I could eventually make my way in my new country.

My excitement, however, was quickly dashed, for this school was not anything like I had imagined. The first problem I encountered was the gangs. These were punk middle school gangs, the baby version of the Bloods and the Crips. I had no idea about gangs or what they were, and I got between the two factions several times. It seemed like both sides competed to see which could make my life the most miserable.

There were police officers on the school grounds and inside the school at all times to help teachers keep the kids under control, but their presence did nothing to ease my mind. Even though police had rescued me, and even though I'd had positive dealings with the court system on the issue of my staying in the United States, I still did not trust authorities. For many years I had been told that the police were bad, and it was hard for me to now see them as the good guys. This meant I was just as nervous about the police presence as I was about the gangs.

Most of the kids in school were not in gangs, but they came from tough backgrounds. These kids were harsh in their language and their actions, which made it hard for quiet me to fit in. I had to adapt quickly. It was the whole "eat or be eaten" scenario, and I'd had more than my share of bullying in my captors' home and in my first foster home. I wasn't going to put up with it anymore. But that was easier to think about than actually accomplish.

Kids of middle school age are hard to be around in the best of circumstances. They are desperate to fit in, and those who do not mold to the cookie-cutter image of everyone else are picked on. That was me. I was the only student in the school who was Muslim. Because my new foster family held tightly to their faith, I had to wear a head covering at school. And I was the only student who did not speak English well. Those two things alone made me the subject of ridicule, and I was taunted, bullied, pushed, pinched, and bruised every day. I tried my best not to cry, because I knew if I did that it would be a huge sign of weakness to the other students, but I couldn't help myself. Most days I broke down well before the lunch hour.

I was put into as many remedial classes as the school staff could find for me, and as far as the other kids were concerned, those classes labeled me as stupid. That's how I became the dumb girl who dressed and talked funny. No one there knew my story, of course, and with this group of kids I am not sure it would have made a difference if they had.

The animosity the other students had for me was building, but so was my anger and resentment toward them. I was angry at life, angry with God, mad at my foster parents for putting me into such a terrible school, mad at my social workers, parents, captors, teachers. I was one angry person, and the rage and hate had been boiling inside me for some time.

Further complicating matters, I did not know why the other kids did not like me. I had done nothing to them. I knew I looked different, talked and dressed differently, but inside I was the same as they were. It was confusing to me and added to my inner turmoil.

One afternoon I was outside, waiting for my foster sister to pick me up after school, when a Hispanic girl spit in my face. This was the worst thing that had happened to me at school, but I sucked it up, wiped the spit off my face, and walked away. However, the girl wouldn't let up. She then called me several names, including "Arab people." I didn't understand what she meant, but her tone of voice let me know what she thought of me. I kept walking.

Finally she came up behind me and pulled my scarf off my head and punched me. That was it, and I let loose. All of my anger and rage came out on her—and I kicked and screamed and punched and scratched with everything I had. When all was said and done, I was in much better shape physically than she was, and while I knew that fighting was not a good way to settle differences, I have to say that afterward I felt great!

The emotions I had unleashed on the girl empowered me. Until that point, I had been a meek young teen. Much of who I was at that time was due to my captivity, and to the abusive men in my life. But no more. I was done being picked on. It was time to step up, for me to demand I be treated as respectfully as anyone else. If I had to do that in a fight, then so be it.

Long term, however, a fight might not have been my best choice, as I was suspended for a week. Most kids in that school would have received a one- or two-day suspension, but the teachers and other staff could see that my anger toward this girl was deep. I had put a lot of bruises on her body, and I bristled with fury anytime her name was mentioned. Because of that I got a full week. I even had to go to Saturday school for a while to make up the days that I'd missed.

After the fight I was enrolled in an Arabic kickboxing class through our mosque. Kickboxing was a way for me to let out my anger in an appropriate way. It made me feel empowered and I liked it a lot, but my foster mom was busy with work and activities for her other kids and rarely had time to take me. After a few sessions I stopped going. I had not had time to make any friends in that class, but what I had been taught stuck with me.

When I returned to my regular classes, it was evident that my teachers were as confused about me as I was. It is an unfortunate fact that the only thing teachers in this school could do was keep some semblance of order. Because the kids were out of control, the teachers got little teaching done. My foster family didn't understand how life was for me there, because the Muslim school their own kids went to was good. The kids in that school behaved themselves and did well on academic tests. This meant my foster parents had no experience or skills to offer me to make my days easier.

While I struggled to fit in during the day, after school I struggled with my homework. Because I was slow to read and understand my studies, most days it took me hours to finish my assignments. Public school was a big change for me, and school had me totally stressed.

Adding to that was the stress I felt in the home of my foster family. I realize now that a home should be a haven, a safe place where you can relax and be yourself. But the dad in this home was as mean as the other Muslim men in my life had been. It was my luck of the draw that here was another Muslim man who did not have much control over his angry feelings.

I thought that Manjit treated his wife and children with little respect. There were many fights, and if Rachel or his daughters spoke out of turn, he'd slap them. His attitude was domineering, and that didn't mix well with my newfound sense of personal empowerment. One area where we clashed was religion. This was a seriously strict Muslim household, which meant the dad and kids got up at four a.m. every morning to say their first prayers. They also often went to the mosque at that early hour to pray. Part of the Muslim religion is to pray five prayers every day at specific times. None of the other homes I had lived in had observed this rule, but this family did.

This family was strict about my wearing the head scarf too.

Because the dad and the brother were not my real dad and brother, I had to wear the head scarf anytime they were in the house, which was often. That was hard for me. I respect women who wear the scarf as a symbol of their purity and their faith. If that is important to you, I fully support you in wearing it, but it wasn't important to me, and when I had to wear it, I hated it.

Many of the Muslim traditions may not have been important for my foster mom either. Her own family was Christian, and because of that my foster dad did not allow his wife to see her own family, didn't even allow them to give her gifts for Christmas. I thought this was terribly sad. Because I had been taken away from my family, I knew how important those ties were. Rachel must have missed her relatives, especially on Christian holidays. Muslim holidays were the only days when she ever went to the mosque.

My foster dad was such a domineering man that I do not know why Rachel stayed with him. I wish she could have spoken up for herself more, and maybe she had earlier in her marriage. Maybe after so many years she just tried to keep as much peace in her home as she could. I was now getting to an age where the issue of standing up for myself was important to me, and the relation ship between my foster parents made me want to become a strong, independent woman.

Manjit had many rules for our home, and one of them was that we were to speak only Arabic inside the house. This didn't make much sense to me. Here I was trying as hard as I could to learn English, and they couldn't support my speaking it at home. No matter the rule, I made the decision to use English only. I was living in an English-speaking country, and I needed to know the language. My decision caused more than one argument, because if someone spoke to me at home in Arabic, I'd answer as best I could in English. Of course, there wasn't that much talking going on inside the house anyway.

Another contradiction was that even though my social workers encouraged me to make friends, I could not bring anyone home, as only those of the Muslim faith were allowed in the house. In fact, I was actively encouraged to stay away from non-Muslims. This didn't make much sense either. I was the only Muslim student in my school, so it was impossible to meet others of my faith.

After school was the best time of the day for me. The school was only a few minutes away from our house, and my foster sister usually picked me up. My foster mom couldn't because she juggled working, and her kids' sports and other after-school schedules. But the older girl had her own car and was usually able to get me. I had to call my foster dad as soon as I got home, though. If I didn't call him a few minutes after school let out, he'd start to call the house, and I'd better have been there. He always dropped me off at school in the morning; maybe he made me call him after school because he wanted to be sure I had stayed at school all day. After the call I'd settle into my room to begin the lengthy process of my homework.

After my homework was finished—and on weekends—I read a lot and watched TV. Most of the books I read were children's books, such as those written by Dr. Seuss. My reading and English language skills were still basic—again, mostly because we spoke Arabic in the home. Those books were special to me, though, especially because my foster dad didn't allow us to go anywhere, so entertainment choices were limited. We did go to Lake Tahoe as a family several times for vacations, and that was a lot of fun. I saw snow for the first time when I was there and totally fell in love with it. Tahoe had deep, deep snow when we were there, and the novelty of being out in it was fun. Even my foster dad relaxed some on those trips, and we had some good times. I wished he could have been that much fun all the time.

Obviously, this family and my relationship with them was complicated. I believe my foster mom and the kids liked me. In fact, my foster dad spoke with my social worker about adopting me, but I didn't want to do that. First, he never talked to me about it but instead went behind my back to try to get the adoption started. It did not help that I did not respect him and didn't agree with the strictness in which he made his family practice their faith. The amount of fighting in the house discouraged me from making this my permanent home, even though I longed for a family to call my own.

Months went by and my anger with my experiences in life only deepened. I began to see another therapist. I had seen one when I was with my first foster family, but even though the speaking in those sessions had been in Arabic, I had not spoken much. I'd been still mistrustful at that point, and far too weighed down by the changes in my life to begin to make any sense of them.

But this time it was different. I was more mature and had the ability to express myself better. I told my therapist how disappointed I was that not a single person from my foster family attended my eighth-grade graduation. It seemed as if every kid had someone there to support them—except me. If my foster family cared about me, as they said they did, why couldn't my foster mom have taken a few hours off from work that day? Why couldn't the older daughter have come? Or my foster dad? I felt miserable on a day that should have been joyful, and that made me mad.

I was finding that I was the kind of person who kept anger bottled up inside. That isn't necessarily a good thing, because people wouldn't even know I was angry with them. We'd have a conversation, something would set me off, and my pent-up anger would spew forth in an explosion of hateful words. Many times when I was in my room, I again asked myself why my parents had sold me into slavery. Why had my captors been cruel to me? What had I ever done to deserve any of what had happened? The questions went round and round in my head, and there were never any answers, and I was filled with a mixture of sadness and anger.

My fury, along with my confused feelings, had troubled me since before I'd been rescued. As I mentioned, at Orangewood I'd been given medicine to help me sleep. Because I'd been extremely anxious about the changes in my life during that time, sleep had been impossible. When I'd been with my first foster family, the medicine prescribed for anxiety and depression had helped balance my moods, which had been all over the place. But the talk part of the therapy had been as helpful, even if I hadn't done very much talking.

I discovered that now that I'd been physically free for a period of time, I was emotionally freer. My small freedoms of being able to go to school and make choices about my spare time at home had done wonders for my state of mind. Now that I was more receptive, my therapist was able to teach me fully how wrong slavery is. I had been told that before but hadn't understood the concept as well as I did now. Through her I learned that it was okay to be mad about my years in captivity. I told her how unhappy I was at school and with my foster family, and she helped me understand more about relationships between people. I had not understood any of those ideas before, and that new knowledge helped me in my interactions with the people around me.

I had never anticipated how difficult it would be to change my mind-set from being a captive to being a free person, or how complicated life could get in the process. Many people in my life thought I should be happy for what I had, happy simply for my freedom, but it wasn't that easy. Happiness is not a switch people can turn off and on. Not that I wasn't happy. In fact, I was thrilled that I no longer had to wait on The Mom and The Dad and their entitled kids. But for many years I had thought I would be happy if only I could see my family. Now I knew that was just a fantasy, and that happiness and disappointment can be tightly intertwined.

My therapist was a nice woman and wanted my foster family to come in for a few sessions, but my foster dad wouldn't allow it. Instead Manjit laughed at me and called me crazy. I knew I wasn't, but I was disappointed that he was closed-minded about the sessions.

My social worker and counselor encouraged me to again talk to my family in Egypt. Because I understood much more about people then, I agreed to give it another try, even though I was not happy about it. The only thing that was different this time around was that my foster dad was able to have several conversations with my biological father. My dad asked my foster family if they could send pictures of me, so I reluctantly dressed in my head scarf and went to a studio my foster family knew and had the pictures taken.

I had a lot of questions for my biological family, but none of them were ever answered. In fact, I never had the opportunity to ask. On the phone I was either being yelled at or was listening to my mom tell me how much she missed me. Something I wondered about was if any of my other siblings had been sold into slavery. I wanted to know if any new brothers or sisters had been born since I had left. And I worried about my mom's health, even though I was furious with her for agreeing to sell me into slavery.

ICE agent Mark Abend had always been there in the background, but he became more active in my life when I was with my second foster family. As time had gone on, some things had changed in the case against my former captors, and he now wanted to see where I was emotionally. Without my cooperation his case would not be as strong, and Mark was definite that he wanted to make these people pay for what they'd done to me. I was fortunate to have him on my side, because few other people would have pursued my former captors with as strong a determination as he did.

Mark flew up from Orange County, and the first time he came, we could actually have a conversation! Before, I had always spoken to Mark through an interpreter, but now we could talk face-to-face. Once that happened, some of my ingrained fear of men fell away, and I realized what a good guy Mark was.

By this time it was May 2004, and I think my strong new personality shocked Mark. Before I had been cowed and depressed whenever I'd been in his presence. Now, several years away from captivity and lots of therapy later, I was in the beginning stages of becoming a capable young woman.

Mark filled me in on the latest events and asked if I wanted to pursue the case. I was just angry enough—and strong enough—to say yes. At that point in my life there was nothing I wanted more than for him to put those people in jail, and to make them responsible for how they'd treated me. My therapist was right: There was nothing right about slavery.

After that I saw and spoke to Mark every few months. He brought two lawyers on board, Robert Keenan and Andrew Kline, along with several members of his Homeland Security team. Together they began the process of bringing justice to me, and to the couple I had thought of for a long time as The Mom and The Dad.

. . .

I was thrilled that the case was moving again, but Rachel and Manjit did not share in my joy. In fact, they encouraged me to drop it and move on with my life. Manjit even asked me to lie about events that had happened when I was in captivity. That pushed me to my limit. I wished he could have lived like I had for years on end. Then we would see if he'd want to "drop it."

Discussion of my participation in the case brought an entirely new round of arguments to my foster home, which led to fights about religious freedom, and many other things. One night at about nine p.m., after an intense argument, my foster dad kicked me out of the house.

"Put on your shoes," he said. "Let's go."

I was not allowed to pack any of my things. He dropped me off at a group home, and it took a week before my social worker could straighten things out. I was heartbroken that I never got to say good-bye to my foster brother and sisters, for I had grown to love them.

In the group home I reverted to my old, quiet self and didn't say much to anyone. All I could think was, *Here we go again,* but at least I was thinking it in English! I wondered why I couldn't find a permanent home, a family who would love me no matter what.

My social worker eventually flew up to get me, and on the plane ride back to Orange County, and ultimately back to Orangewood, I said, "I do not want to be placed in another Muslim home. I am done with that." I didn't realize then that people of other faiths could be mean too, but I didn't want any part of another domi-neering Muslim man in my life.

While I wanted to be with the right family, I was fine living at Orangewood until that happened. My friend Autumn was there again too, and this time I could even talk with her some in English. Her "wild side" kept her in trouble, but I found her to be an interesting person who had repeated placements with the same foster parents.

Orangewood is well run, and I easily fit back into life there. One reason I think their system runs as smoothly as it does is their point system. If you behaved well, you earned points. If you earned enough points, you got a reward. Some of the rewards included bowling or shopping, but during the time I was there one reward was to go to an Anaheim Angels baseball game. We had our own special area for seating, and while I didn't understand the game, why we cheered when we did, or anything about what was going on, I loved every second of it. That game turned me into a lifelong Angels fan, and I still love going to their games.

On the placement side, while I wanted a family, I knew I had several strikes against me. The older a child gets, the harder he or she is to place. I was fifteen now but still far behind socially and in school. I prepared to wait, but I hoped with everything I had that I would find a real home and a loving family.

CHAPTER TEN

I didn't have to wait too long before I got my wish. Not too long after I turned fifteen, I was placed in the home of a family in Orange, about sixty-five miles from Orangewood's location.

When my prospective mom and her youngest daughter first came to Orangewood to meet me, I was jaded by my previous foster care experiences and did not hold out much hope that this situation would be any different. I did not want to be labeled as a "difficult child," though, so I put on my happy face for the meeting. I was glad to realize, however, that my social worker had heard my words, because this family was not Muslim.

The way foster parenting works is that the parents are paid by the state for every child they take in. Payment varies from state to state, and from each individual referring organization. I believe that foster parents of kids from Orangewood got paid a bit more than many others, because Orangewood was a good organization that tried hard to place kids in the right homes. Maybe the people who made such decisions thought the extra money would attract parents who might otherwise not be interested in fostering. In talking to other kids at Orangewood, I found that the sad reality was that this system brought in some prospective parents who were there only for the money. I sat in front of this woman and her daughter and hoped that was not the reason they were there. There was no way to know until I learned more, and the only way to do that was to spend a few days with them.

My prospective foster mom and her youngest daughter picked me up, and I went to spend a weekend with their family. I learned that the family had had foster kids in the past—and that they were taking care of the dad's nephew plus their three biological children. If I stayed, I would become the fifth child in the home, and the oldest. The nephew was ten, and then there was a boy of seven, followed by two girls who were six and four. They seemed nice, including the dad, but by I now realized what a huge decision this was. I had found that moving in with a new family could be the answer to my dreams. It could also become my worst nightmare.

On Monday my social worker gathered my things from Orangewood and came out to the house. When she got there, she saw the indecision on my face and said, "You can either stay here or you can come back to Orangewood with me, but you have to make a decision now."

I went back to Orangewood. Part of my decision was based on fear. What if this family turned out to be as bad as my previous ones? Another part of my choice was based on my gut feeling. My intuition told me that something was up with this family, but I could not put my finger on it. Not to mention that there were no kids near my age and I had hoped to find a family that had some kids I could bond with closely.

My next few days were spent at Orangewood, but when a staff member said, "No other family is in sight for you," I went back to this new family. My new foster mom and the youngest daughter again picked me up, and on the way back we stopped for lunch at an upscale family burger place. Then we went to my new home.

I have to say that the house was beautiful. It was located in a wealthier area of town and had four bedrooms. My new foster mom and dad, Patty and Steve, shared the master bedroom. Steve was tall and had the looks of a television anchor. Patty was short, like me, but blond. The nephew and oldest son roomed together, the two girls were together, and there was a room for me. There was a large open area in the home that no one seemed to use, and a living room that opened to the kitchen, which was where everyone hung out.

Not too long after I arrived another foster kid was brought into the family. This girl was two or three years younger than I was and was a deeply troubled child. In the years that I was with this family there were dozens of girls like her who were in and out of the house. Most stayed a matter of weeks, although several stayed a few months. All of them roomed with me. For these girls my family was a transition family to see if the girl was ready to go back to her real mom and dad, or if she needed to be put into permanent placement.

Each girl was between the ages of eleven and thirteen, and each changed the family dynamic with her presence. This was a bit unsettling, especially when the new girl had serious behavior problems, as some did. But others were sweet. In either case the reality was that by the time I got to know a new foster sister, she was gone. This did nothing for my issues with trust, nor did it help me bond with others. In fact, the situation did the opposite. It got to the point where I didn't even want to try to get to know any new girl. Because if I did and I liked her, then my heart would be ripped out when she left.

My relationship with the nephew was challenging but in a different way. He seemed resentful of the time and attention Patty and Steve gave to me. If I did the smallest thing wrong, or if I forgot to do something, he was sure to tell his uncle and aunt. Very little got by this kid because he was always watching me.

I liked the other kids, though, the seven-year-old boy and the four- and six-year-old girls. These younger siblings reminded me of the younger brothers and sisters I had left behind in Egypt. I missed them beyond words, but in the years since I had left the home of my captors, I had forgotten even more about my siblings. Now I found that I loved being a big sister again! These were good kids, and we had a lot of fun together.

Steve was a good provider, and the love he showed to his kids made me revise my frosty opinion of the male species. Maybe, in addition to Mark Abend, there were good men in the world. My foster dad showed genuine concern for each kid who lived under his roof and often asked me if I was okay. He let me know I could always talk to him if I had a problem, and I appreciated that so much. Few other people had ever done that for me, and I often took him up on his offer.

But he and my foster mom did not get along. That was the odd thing about this family that I had not been able to put my finger on at first. In my previous homes the dad had always been the aggressor. In this home it was my foster mom.

Patty and Steve battled frequently, and it often got out of hand. I saw her chuck a bottle of hair spray at his face. She yelled a lot and had no friends that I knew about. And her spending habits were the cause of many of their arguments. The battles over money made me feel that my foster mom wanted me around only for the money. That was not a good feeling to have, so I withheld my feelings for her and enjoyed spending time with the three youngest members of the family.

Even though life in my first two foster homes, and to some extent at Orangewood, had been hard, I had learned a lot and made great strides. For example, now, for the first time, one of my social workers was a man. While I still worked with my social worker from Orangewood, I guess the new county I lived in felt I was far enough away from my Muslim upbringing to feel confident enough to talk with a man who did not live in my home. And you know what? They were right. I liked this guy. He knew my foster family from other foster kids who had been in the home, and he was an exceptionally nice person. He was a good advocate for me, and I greatly enjoyed our sessions.

Unfortunately, I thought my new therapist was the worst ever. I was afraid that she was passing everything I said on to Patty, and I felt I could not talk about my feelings without fear that my words would come to slap me in the face. This was disappointing because my previous therapist had been quite helpful and I had been hoping for more of the same.

Before too long I made the decision to stop therapy. Why waste time when something was not beneficial? Plus, I had become pretty good at talking about my feelings with people I felt close to, especially Mark and my social worker.

That fall, the fall I was sixteen, I entered high school as a sophomore. I was lucky, as this was an excellent school filled with talented, caring teachers. I had finally caught up enough in my studies to somewhat keep up with my classes, even though I was placed in a remedial English class. But I had a regular English class too. Progress!

At home Steve and Patty's fighting wore me down, and I tried to stay as far away from it as possible. When my social worker surprised me with my Social Security card and said, "Now that you have this card, you can get a job, and a driver's license, too, if you want," I thought of the perfect solution. If I had a license, I could drive. And if I could drive, I could get a job—a job that would keep me out of the house and away from my foster parents' fights.

I had been craving independence for what seemed like an eternity, and the freedom that came with driving could provide me with some of that. The written test, though, was difficult for me. In fact, I failed it three times. While I could read English pretty well by this time, the way this test was written, many of the questions did not make sense to me. Finally a lady at the testing station asked if English was my second language. When I said, "Yes, it is," she said there was an option where someone could read the test to me. Wow, what a difference that made. The fourth time I took the test I got 100 percent.

Patty and Steve had a huge, old white Honda that they let me drive. It drove like a truck, but I didn't care. The next day I drove to the mall, walked around, and filled out job applications at several different places. I knew my choices would be limited. The job market was tough anyway, but without previous work experience I knew it would be nearly impossible for me to find employment. The way entry-level jobs were then—and possibly still are—college grads were taking many jobs that had previously been filled by high school students.

But a few days later Godiva Chocolatier called me in for an interview. I was nervous about talking to a stranger who essentially held the keys to my future in her hands. I interviewed with a nice female manager, however, and several days later she called me to tell me I got the job! I couldn't wait to get started.

I now had wheels *and* a job. How cool was that? I soon began a new morning routine. On the way to class I'd stop at a gas station and pick up some Flamin' Hot Cheetos and a Monster Energy drink that I bought with my own money that I had earned. Once in a while I'd add some cream cheese to dip the Cheetos in. Yum, that was my "healthy" breakfast. For lunch I'd buy some SunChips and a huge chocolate chip cookie at the school cafeteria that I'd munch on throughout the rest of day. A few months earlier I had decided to stop eating meat. For some reason it no longer appealed to me. But, even though I was a vegetarian, I wasn't eating many vegetables.

One thing I liked about high school was that several of my teachers treated me just as they did everyone else. It seems like such a small thing, but to me it was huge. This kind of treatment had been a long time coming, and I can't tell you how glad I was to be considered a regular student, rather than someone people didn't know what to do with.

My social skills had improved some, but there were still many things that I did not understand. I could not figure out why a lot of kids acted bratty and were disrespectful toward their teachers. Why did my fellow students not do their homework? Why did they complain about their mother dropping them off, as if it were the worst thing in the world? Didn't they realize what a wonderful opportunity school was? Education is a gift that people here in the United States enjoy freely, but I know firsthand that the process of learning is not available to everyone in other parts of the world.

Education opens doors to opportunities. No matter what your dream is, it will be easier to achieve if you have the foundation of knowledge. I have always considered school an opportunity to make myself a better person and have never understood why others do not see it that way too. That was and is one of my biggest adjustments to life since my rescue. Why do people not appreciate what they have? Why do they cheat themselves out of a better life by not doing their homework and learning the subject matter?

Despite my thoughts about the other kids, I found I was developing a few friendships. Interestingly enough, my name helped make that possible. Shyima is an unusual name here in the United States, and it isn't that common in Egypt, either. Shyima was the name of the sister of the prophet Muhammad, and out of respect, custom has it that only special babies can have the name, which means "strong-willed." The uniqueness of my name made it easy for my teachers and the other students to know who I was.

It helped too that my English was now passable. Most people understood me, and I understood them. Learning the language of my new country had been a long, slow process, but it had been totally worth it. It's hard to make lasting friendships or understand why things are the way they are when you cannot communicate.

Life was getting better, but inside I was still a jaded person. I can look back now and see that I wasn't the friendliest person to be around, but my history was that the vast majority of the people in my life had not treated me well. Because of that my ongoing issues with trust were still with me.

One person who helped me gain trust was my new friend Amber Bessix. We went to the same high school, and although I had seen her in passing in the hallway, we had not spoken before we met through work. Amber and I became a great team at Godiva, and she went on to become one of my best friends.

I liked my job, even though I hadn't specifically been interested in a retail store position. Meeting new people and having pride in a job well done were extra bonuses. I found too that when someone who wore traditional Egyptian clothing, or spoke a bit of Arabic, came into the store, I was instantly brought back to my early years with my family. In that way my job offered a small but comforting piece of home.

Since then every job I have had has been in a retail store. Unfortunately, the hours I spent on my feet at work were hard on my rheumatoid arthritis. I had been diagnosed with RA after I'd come to live with my new foster family. During my sophomore year of high school I had scary swellings on my body and raised bubbles on my knees, and my joints were so painful that I was limited in what I could do. Plus, my muscles would get tight and I often couldn't move in the morning. On some days I had many sharp pains and couldn't go to school. In fact, I was often so stiff that it would take me hours to get up and out of bed.

Even though I had been telling my doctor and my foster parents about my symptoms, not a single person took me seriously. "You're fine. You're just being a teen," my doctor said. This man treated a lot of kids in foster care. I don't know if he thought we weren't worth his full concern and attention, but the way he dismissed me bordered on rude.

To make matters worse, my symptoms worsened as I grew older. One day I realized I had dropped twenty-five pounds in a short period of time. "I can't eat," I said to Patty. "I can't move." My foster parents followed the doctor's lead and did not think that anything was wrong with me. I didn't speak to my foster mom for three weeks. I was that mad!

Eventually Steve qualified for better insurance, and as soon as I could, I took the initiative to find a new doctor on my own. When the tests came back, my new doctor told me that not only did I have rheumatoid arthritis, but my disease was advanced enough that my joints looked like those of a woman in her eighties. While I was not pleased to find that I had RA, I was comforted that there was actually a name for what I had been experiencing. Until then, I'd had no idea what was wrong with me.

The diagnosis was a huge relief, because now that my doctor and I knew what we were dealing with, we could develop a plan to treat it. The first step in that plan was for me to go to a specialist. He was extremely helpful, and I regularly saw this physician until a few months ago, when he retired. Among many other things, he showed me how my knees and wrists were the most affected parts of my body. I was glad to hear this, because I had been telling people for a long time how much these joints hurt.

The medication I was now taking for RA was hard to adjust to, especially because I had not yet discontinued the medications

I had been taking for years for insomnia, depression, and anxiety. With all of the meds combined I ended up with mouth sores and hair loss. But I quickly gained back the weight I'd lost—and then some!

During this process my doctor asked for my parental and family medical histories. I had none of that. At times I don't want to tell people about my past, and for some reason this was one of those times. In lieu of the truth I told him I had never met my biological family. My social worker then went the extra mile to try to find some information for me, but there was no information to be had. That is another sad fact of slavery, of human trafficking. Other people will be able to take specific preventative steps toward good health if, for example, they know breast cancer or strokes run in their family. I will probably not have that opportunity.

RA is not curable, but treatment can make a world of difference in how well a person feels and how much they are able to do physically. Now that I know warmth helps my joints, I often take long, hot baths. I have never done well in cold weather and can see how fortunate I was to have ended up in California rather than Maine, Montana, or Minnesota.

Today I still take medication, but I also get steroid shots in my hips every two months. It helps if I stay active with gentle exercise, so I walk as much as I can. Left untreated, RA will take a lot of out of you. I know it did me. That's why I am careful to take extra good care of my body now.

Sometime after my diagnosis I made the decision to stop taking the other medications I had been taking. The insomnia medicine, the medication for anxiety, and the prescription for depression: gone. All of it. I stopped because I did not like the way they made me feel, and even I could see that I was too quiet and too withdrawn when I was on the meds.

I believe under certain circumstances that taking medication under the supervision of a doctor or therapist can be helpful. I also believe that those prescriptions helped me tremendously early on. After I was rescued and into my years with my first two foster families I was too nervous, anxious, and depressed to function well. But now I was no longer that intimidated young girl. For me, the medication did what it was supposed to do, and then I was done with it. Besides, it was way too much with the addition of the medications for my arthritis.

The big concern I had about having RA was that because of it I might not be able to go into my career choice: law enforcement. From the day I had been rescued, I had wanted to help others like me—people who were held in captivity. I later found that my RA would not affect my goal, but that small scare made me focus on taking the first step toward my dream, and that was to become a citizen of the United States.

CHAPTER ELEVEN

All throughout this time legal battles were brewing for my former captors. Mark Abend was a frequent visitor and often drove me back to Orange County to meet with prosecutors. By now I looked forward to these sessions because with each meeting I felt The Mom and The Dad were that much closer to getting what was due them. What goes around comes around.

There were many interviews, and the officials kept me up to date about their plans to bring me justice. At one point they asked if they could use a letter I had written to my former captors. I don't know if The Mom and The Dad ever saw the letter, but my therapist thought it would help me if I wrote it. Now Mark and his team thought it would help the case if the judge could see it. I am not sure of the date of the letter, but from the style of my writing, I was probably about sixteen. Here is what I wrote:

Hi,

My name is Shyima Hassan. I have a big family in Egypt,
five brothers and five sisters. I had the best brothers and sisters
in Egypt. I had the best time being with them. I loved them
so much because they loved me back and they made life easy for
me. When I needed someone they were there for me.

I also had friends in Egypt. I had this person that was there
for me, that I played with. Yes, I had friends, too, like everyone
else. I also had a mom and a dad who loved me before you
blackmailed them and you made them give me up. That was
the day I thought life was over, and you know why? Because
you took me away from my life. That's when I also lost faith
in God. You guys made me lose my one true love in the world
because of all the things you guys told my family and the things
you did to me.

You made my life miserable and you did not care. You guys
treated me like crap in Egypt and in the U.S.A. I had to keep
my mouth shut because of what you said you would do to my
sister. And, yes, I am away from my family because of what you
said she did. So I had to deal with you because I love my sister
and would not want to see her in jail. You not only blackmailed
my mom and dad, you blackmailed my heart.

*Now I have a better way of life away from you guys. I have a
great family. I am almost done with high school, too. Life is just
great without you guys and I know I have God with me, too.
I am living my life like a real teenager and everyday I thank
God and everyone else who saved me away from you.*

I was surprised to learn that Mark was so determined to see
The Mom and The Dad pay for what they'd done to me that he
was going to fly all the way to Egypt to meet my parents. I think
he hoped to get facts to back up the prosecution's case. I tried to
prepare him as to the kind of people he might find, but even so, he
must have been quite taken aback when he met my family.

Mark later told me that when he met with my mom and dad, a
lawyer and a stenographer were there. It sounded as if my parents
were afraid they might get into trouble and wanted to be sure
the meeting was recorded in a legal fashion. I believe that The
Dad paid for these services for my parents. Mark said that at the
meeting my dad looked quite frail and in poor health. My dad
told Mark that he'd recently had open heart surgery and that my
captor, The Dad, had paid for that, too.

Mark must have been astounded at the lack of compassion my
parents showed. Even after this much time, rather than saying,
"We miss Shyima. We love her. When can we see her?" they made
it clear to Mark that they wanted me to go back to my captors.

I have to hope that some of that was their not understanding that what they'd done to me was wrong. Most of us enjoy a decent standard of living here in the United States, but it was not unusual for poor families in Egypt to sell their children into service to a wealthier family.

My parents, I think, saw their children as income opportunities. My mom and dad had so little that in their eyes everyone needed to contribute financially, even the kids. My placement with The Mom and The Dad had brought my family about one hundred Egyptian pounds every month. At the time, that converted roughly to seventeen US dollars. Many families in the US spend more than that for a meal at McDonald's.

I had always been told that most of my "wages" had gone to repay what my sister had stolen. How much could it have been? Even with the debt of honor thrown in, I believe I was held by my captors long after my sister's debt had been repaid.

Through Mark I learned that by this time my parents were living in a dirt house, which meant that whatever money they'd lost when I'd been rescued was missed. And through pictures that he either took or was given, I could see that my family's clothes were as dirty and worn as they had been when I was taken away from them. But you know what? It didn't matter. It had not been my choice to leave my family. I was not given the option to stay, and I can tell you that if I had been given the choice, I never would have left my loved ones. It didn't matter that we had next to nothing. We had love for one another, and when all is said and done, love is the only thing that is important in life. That my captors' home had been nicer than my family's was of no importance to me. Not many would trade a nice house for twenty-hour work days, no pay, no vacations or days off, no medical care, being slapped, and continually being told that you are stupid. Even now I get angry just thinking about it.

My sister was willing to testify on behalf of my captors too, the sister who'd stolen. After hearing this I can only assume that she had been told either by my dad or their lawyer what to say. "They treated me very well when I was there," she said over and over again in her videotaped pretrial interview. If that was the case, then why had she stolen from them?

After that it was "hurry up and wait." Again, I was learning that the legal process in the United States takes a long time. While I waited, I kept busy at work and going to school, but I didn't tell many people what was going on. For the most part I kept my former life private. Especially at school. Even though I knew a trial was looming that could potentially bring me a great deal of personal satisfaction, few people outside my family knew about it. Part of that was because I wanted to be a regular kid. The other part was that the last thing in the world I wanted to do was see The Mom and The Dad again. But when the time came for me to confront them, I did.

I so badly wanted my former captors convicted that I could taste it, but speaking up against The Mom and The Dad with them in the room was one of the hardest things I ever did. I was glad

Mark was there to help me through this unpleasant task. My foster dad was supportive, but I always thought first of Mark whenever the word "dad" popped into my brain. I am still blown away that Mark spent so much time over many years to try to convict The Mom and The Dad. He didn't have to do it, and honestly, most others would not have.

Early on in the proceedings Robert Keenan and Andrew Kline had been assigned to my case. I needed two lawyers because they each handled different areas of the law, and this case was complex enough that there was a lot of legal ground to cover. Robert was based in Los Angeles, and Andrew in Washington, DC. Both men prepped me for the trial and took me through many last-minute changes. I hated revisiting the terrible memories in the depth that we did, but I knew it was the only way to make these people pay. I had no notion of what that "pay" might amount to in terms of jail time, but I hoped it would involve a long stay behind bars. I knew, though, that the more information Mark and the lawyers had, the better chance we would have of a conviction and a strong sentence.

One of the things I had to do was watch video footage that had been taken while I'd been in captivity. This was a tense process for me. The footage had been seized along with other documents and records, not long after I had been rescued. While I watched, Mark and my lawyers asked question after question about what was going on with the family when each video was shot. Who was in the video? What were they doing? Saying? And most important: Where was I?

We wanted to show through video that I had not been part of the family. The Mom and The Dad were apparently going to claim that I had been. In one video the family is celebrating their youngest daughter's birthday. All of the family members are shown seated at a table in the dining room and are surrounded by plates, cups, glasses, silverware, and food. There is a lot of food. I pop in and out of the video as I hurriedly clear plates from the table, bring more water, and place other food out for people to eat. If I was part of the family, then why wasn't I seated at the table having a good time like everyone else?

I was surprised to learn that my biological family had consented to being filmed for a video. In it many members of my family stated how much they loved and missed me, and how they wished I were back home with them. That video was the hardest for me to watch. I had many mixed emotions, but mostly, looking at the footage made me feel sad inside. Then I thought of the many times my dad had yelled at me for not going back with my captors, and all the times my mom had told me I had to stay. I thought too of my sister who had changed the course of my life with her actions.

Eventually I began to cry. Mark was in the room with me, as were Robert and Andrew. Mark gave the lawyers a look, and they stepped away. Then Mark sat next to me and tried to give me courage. "It doesn't matter what they say," he said. "These people aren't in your life anymore. You have a lot of support here; *do not* let these people bring you down."

He was right, but more than what my family said on the video, the saddest part of watching my family was that, other than my mom and dad, I didn't remember any of the people. How wrong is that? I should have recognized every person caught on camera. I should have known how my mother moved, how my sister tilted her head. But I didn't. I didn't recall any of it, or any of them. All I could recognize was that my mother looked much older, and my dad, who had always been small and thin, had lost even more weight.

On the surface it looked like this should have been a pretty open-and-shut case. My captors had held me against my will, which is a violation of many different laws, both state and federal. But a case like this, I learned, is never easy. Initially there are jurisdictional issues to settle. Which law enforcement agency gets to prosecute, and for which particular crime? Then there is the fact that in the United States we operate on a system of innocent until proven guilty. Everyone here has the right to an attorney, and once The Mom and The Dad lawyered up, their legal team did everything they could to delay justice. It is amazing how many kinks one side in a legal battle can throw into the mix.

Mark, my lawyers, and I prepared over and over for the trial. I was extremely nervous about it. I didn't want to have to go through that, to sit in a courtroom day after day and look at those people who'd stolen my childhood. But I was ready for it and would have done it. However, at the last minute The Mom and The Dad both pled guilty. I guess even their lawyers could see that the evidence against them was strong enough that my captors were certain to go to jail. The only thing up in the air was which jail and for how long. The Mom and The Dad's legal team must have advised them that they'd never win in a jury trial, and that their sentences would be lighter if they pled guilty.

I was not there when they gave their pleas, but I later heard that the judge cried. I am beyond glad that people who can make a difference saw through my captors' lies.

The guilty plea meant that I would not have to sit in the courtroom like a specimen for my former captors to view. I only had to sit in the gallery (the audience part of the courtroom) for the sentencing hearing. The purpose of a sentencing hearing is to determine what punishment the defendant deserves for the crime he or she committed. Witnesses can be called at the hearing by both sides, which helps the judge better decide on the appropriate punishment. Defendants can speak on their own behalf, and the people they have wronged have the opportunity to address them. This meant that I had the chance to say anything I wanted to The Mom or The Dad and they had to sit there and take it.

At one point I might have jumped at this opportunity. I certainly had a lot to say to these two people who had taken everything from me. But now I wanted to get it over with. I despised my former captors with such a passion that I didn't want to use up any energy on them. They simply were not worth my time. All I wanted was to sit in the audience and see for myself that The Mom and The Dad were finally going to get what was coming to them. That was enough for me.

. . .

On the big day I rode with Steve and Patty to the courthouse in Orange County. I was nervous and felt sick to my stomach. I hadn't seen The Mom or The Dad in many years, and of all the people in the world, those were the two people I least wanted to see.

When we got to the courtroom, I could see The Mom and The Dad in the front on the right side of the room. Many of their friends, and members of their extended family, sat near them. In fact, the entire right side was filled with their supporters.

Mark, Robert, and Andrew sat up front on the left, and I sat with Steve and Patty in the middle of the room behind them. The only other people on our side were reporters. I have no idea how they knew to come, but there were a number of them there.

Even though The Mom and The Dad occasionally glanced around the room, as did many of their supporters, I do not think any of them recognized me. And why should they? Besides the fact that I was almost a high school graduate rather than an uneducated child, my entire demeanor had changed. Instead of a meek, browbeaten kid, I was an up-front young woman who could hold my own almost anywhere. But I would rather have been just about anywhere other than there. I wanted justice, but I knew the next minutes were going to be as emotionally tough as any I had ever experienced.

The Mom was the first to take the stand. I had been told that she had been taking English classes, but she still spoke through a translator. I remembered enough Arabic to understand her, though. I understood quite clearly the first hate-filled words out of her mouth. "I can't believe you would hold this hearing on a holy day when I should be home with my children," she spit.

The hearing did take place on a minor Muslim holy day, but what set me off was that I hadn't seen my family in almost nine years, and The Mom was complaining that she wasn't at home with her family for a day. How dare she!

Then The Mom said regarding me, "If I had asked her if she wanted to go home and she had said she did, that's the first thing I would have done, but I never asked her."

That statement sent me over the top. I had asked over and over to go home. She had been there when I'd been on the phone with my parents and had cried and begged to be allowed to return to my family. I began to stew and squirm, and before too long Mark noticed my distress and handed me a pen and a piece of paper. I slapped words onto that paper as fast as I could.

I almost jumped out of my seat when The Mom said, "I fed her, clothed her, and treated her as I did my own children." Really? I never saw her biological children sleeping in the garage, washing their clothes in a bucket, or cooking, cleaning, or doing laundry. For goodness' sake, I'd even had to put the toothpaste on her children's toothbrushes. I was furious that The Mom took no responsibility for ruining my childhood. None.

The only time she showed any break in her outraged attitude was when she was asked why she had not put me in school. Then she wavered and offered a variety of excuses that didn't make much sense to anyone.

The Dad didn't say much when his turn came to take the stand. Except he did say, "I want to apologize to Shyima." Mark and some others thought he showed a bit of compassion, but I thought the words were only delivered in the hopes of getting his sentence reduced. In the years I had lived in his house, I had gotten pretty good at reading his body language.

I had not planned to speak. Did not want to speak. But, after The Mom and The Dad were through, Mark turned to me with a questioning look on his face, and I jumped out of my chair and went to the front of the room. From the expressions on everyone's faces, I think that was the first time anyone on my captors' side knew that I was there.

"I can't believe she said what she did about today being a holiday," I shouted. "I haven't seen my family in nine years because of her. You want to talk about stepping on people? Well, she steps. They never treated me as their daughter. Never. Where was their loving when it came to me? Wasn't I a human being too? I slept in the garage without a light and waited on them hand and foot even when I was sick. I felt like I was nothing when I was with them. What they did to me will affect me for the rest of my life, and I am far, far better off without them."

Then I began to cry. Andrew came to me and comforted me as he led me back to my seat. I hated that I had enough anger pent up inside me that I was crying. I hated that I had to be there on that day. I hated the arrogant, superior look in The Mom's eyes. And I hated the act of human trafficking more than I could say. Slavery, by any word, is wrong.

Minutes later the judge revealed his decision. The Dad was sentenced to three years. The Mom got twenty-one months, which was equal to the time I'd been held against my will in their house here in the United States. On top of the sentences, they were ordered to pay me $76,137. This amount was equivalent to what they would have paid me if I'd earned minimum wage for the estimated number of hours that I "worked" for them after I came to the United States. I was excited about the money, as that was a sizable sum, but I was disappointed in the length of the sentences. I had hoped The Mom and The Dad would have to remain behind bars for a much longer time.

My disappointment did not last long, however, because Mark had a surprise in store for me. Before anyone could leave the courtroom, the doors were closed and locked. Then The Mom and The Dad were escorted out into the hallway. Soon after, Mark asked me to follow. I didn't know what to expect and was confused, but I trusted that Mark would not let anything bad happen to me.

In the hall I found The Mom and The Dad surrounded by ICE agents. Mark had been with me as a friend, but he had called his colleagues from Immigration and Customs Enforcement because the temporary visas for The Mom and The Dad had long since expired. They were both here in the country illegally.

"I wanted you to see this," said Mark as officials clamped hand-cuffs on The Mom and The Dad. The Dad just stood there, but The Mom began to scream.

And me? I had a huge smile on my face. This was the best scene ever! The horrified expressions on the faces of The Mom and The Dad were priceless. I even got to see them being patted down in a weapons search. The next thing I knew their twin boys were there. I didn't recognize them at first; they had grown that much. Plus, it was hard to see what they looked like as they were crying and yelling as hard and as loud as The Mom and The Dad. Even the family's lawyers were shouting. All in all it was quite a sight.

Mark and my attorneys were pumped. I was pumped! Our years and years of hard work had paid off, and my captors got what they deserved. The outcome did a lot to restore my faith in human decency. Everyone from the judge on down had seen what an injustice I had been dealt during my life with these people. Not only that, these kind officials had taken steps to correct it. That, in my book, was huge.

When we headed to the elevator, a reporter from the *Los Angeles Times* approached me to ask for an interview. "No, thank you," I said. I had too many emotions rolling around inside me and couldn't begin to focus on anything like that. But Patty insisted, so I agreed to meet the reporter at a small restaurant next to the courthouse. On the way to the elevator, though, attorneys for The Mom and The Dad pulled themselves together enough to try to stop us. "We only want to talk," one of them said. "Maybe this was all a misunderstanding."

Before I even knew what was happening, Mark, Robert, and Andrew shut them down. "You cannot come near her," one of them said. "You cannot speak to her, and no, you cannot ride in the same elevator with her."

I did the interview with the reporter even though I was mad that Patty insisted that I do it. I wished that she had respected my wishes on this, of all days. I was especially upset because she seemed to revel in the attention, rather than letting me have my day.

Later Mark sent me photos of The Mom and The Dad in jail. Each wore an orange jumpsuit, and I have to say, orange is not The Mom's best color. Those photos did two things for me. First, they made me feel, more than ever, that I wanted to be in law enforcement. The system had worked well for me, and I wanted to be the person who helped make it work for someone else.

Second, the photos were a big visual reminder that the case was over and my captors were not going anywhere anytime soon. That was a huge relief to me, and for the first time since I had been taken from my family, I felt relaxed inside. I could breathe.

CHAPTER TWELVE

After I had been with Steve and Patty awhile, a foster girl of about ten came to stay. She hadn't been there long when she told a teacher that something bad had happened to her while she was at our house. Her teacher followed up by calling the girl's social worker. There were a number of interviews and conversations that resulted in the girl's being taken out of our home.

The entire situation made me mad, because even though Steve and Patty had their faults, nothing bad had happened to that girl while she'd stayed with us. I am not sure why the girl lied, but quite soon after that, social workers began to talk of taking me out of the home too. I didn't want that, because I finally was beginning to settle in. I didn't want to go back to Orangewood, didn't want to go through the emotional upheaval of leaving my foster brother and sisters and settling in with a new family.

That's when my social worker said to Patty, Steve, and me, "You know, a move could be prevented if you"—she nodded at my foster parents—"obtained guardianship over Shyima. Shyima, what do you think about that? Would you like to stay with Steve and Patty?"

I nodded that I would. I thought it was a good idea. But then even better news came.

"Now, if you adopt Shyima," my social worker continued, "she could obtain citizenship and be a real citizen of the United States."

Becoming a United States citizen had become a dream of mine. By now the US was my home, and my days of wanting to go "home" to Egypt were far behind me. When the social worker told us that any child of a citizen of the United States becomes a citizen too, I agreed to go ahead with the adoption.

My social workers had been such a help to me. From helping me adapt to life here in the United States, to being sure my needs were met, they had become people I could count on over and over again. A social worker at Orangewood had helped me apply for and get both my green card and my Social Security card. That had allowed me to receive medical care, among many other services. I was glad that safety net was there, for there was no one else to provide it for me. Over time I had learned to trust my social workers as they navigated me through many complex systems.

To their credit Steve and Patty were not opposed to the idea of adopting me. My concern was that this couple fought often, and I wasn't sure I wanted to be a bigger part of the family than I already was, even though I had fallen in love with my younger foster brother and sisters.

But if the adoption helped me obtain citizenship, then I was okay with it. My desire to become a real part of my new country outweighed any unsettled feelings I had about my foster family, and I went ahead with it. The process was surprisingly simple. Several social workers filled out some paperwork for my foster parents to sign, and then a court date was scheduled.

On the big day Steve, Patty, and I went to the county courthouse. On the way my soon-to-be new mom and dad had a huge fight. Patty was mad at the world because the shirt she'd wanted to wear had not been cleaned properly, and Steve and I had to listen to her loud complaints throughout the hour or more it took us to get to the courthouse. I was angry at her—and at Steve, too, because he never stepped up to tell her how ridiculous she was acting.

Over the years, Mark Abend had become the closest thing I had to family, and he met us there. I was happy that he could share this special day with me. Plus, he was a nice buffer between my argumentative foster parents and me.

Inside the courtroom the judge let me sit in her chair. That was pretty cool. Then the judge said, "Steve and Patty, do you agree to treat Shyima as your own and provide for her as you would your natural born children?" Patty and Steve both said, "Yes, we will." Then, before I even realized what was happening, the judge signed the order, we took some pictures with her, and boom, there I was with real parents and a real family.

To celebrate we went to eat at a nice French restaurant. Mark could not come, but some of my new extended family came. All of the fighting from earlier in the day was forgotten, and it was one of the nicest times I had ever had.

I thought I would feel differently when the adoption was completed because I was now legally part of a family, but I didn't. My new mom and dad still fought. Their nephew, my new cousin, still didn't like me much; and I still had RA, went to school, and worked. Life went on. I just had a new name.

I was born Shyima El-Sayed Hassan, but when I learned that I had the opportunity to change my name during the adoption process, I did. I changed my middle name to Janet-Rathiba. "Janet" was after Patty's grandmother. She was a wonderfully sweet woman whom I adored. "Rathiba" was after my own grandmother, the one far away in Egypt whom I had loved. I didn't know whether or not she was alive, but I wanted to honor the love she had for me by taking her name. In retrospect, I am surprised that I recalled her name. I had forgotten the names of many others who'd been important to me when I'd lived with my biological family.

A short time after I was adopted, I called a number that was on a piece of paper I had been given when I'd gotten my green card. The number was to inquire about obtaining citizenship, and I was filled with giddy excitement as I made the call. Sadly, my hopes were dashed when I found out that my social worker had been mistaken. I could have automatically become a citizen only if I had been adopted before I'd turned sixteen. I'd recently had my seventeenth birthday and was now told that I had to wait until I was eighteen before I could apply for citizenship. I would also have to undergo a lengthy interview and take a detailed test.

The time frame turned out to be much longer, though. It turned out that I could apply for citizenship five years after I got my green card, and then only if I had not been convicted of any crimes. I had not received my green card until I was fifteen.

I was devastated to learn this. First my heart sank into my stomach, and then my thoughts turned bitter. "What else could I expect?" I said to myself. "Other people never, ever get it right when it comes to me." I can't say that I was mad at the social worker, but I was discouraged. I wanted more than anything to belong to my new country. After a few days of being in the dumps, though, I sucked it up. *If I have to wait three years,* I thought, *I will.* Better late than never.

I had stopped any pretense of being Muslim when I'd moved to my adoptive family's home, because I had gotten so tired of every foster family forcing the Muslim religion on me. I had studied the Koran with my first and second set of foster parents. The dads of those families had usually read it aloud, and a line that stuck with me said something to the effect of "You respect me." This was a reference to adult men. From my perspective, however, adult Muslim men had done nothing worthy of my respect. I felt that the demand for respect without earning it was hypocritical. I experienced that demand over and over during my early years and wanted no more part of it. I was more than ready for something new.

My new family belonged to a Christian community church, and I began attending services there. Although I didn't always agree with the pastor's politics, I liked him as a person and know he always acted out of compassion for others. I attended my friend Amber's church too, which was also Christian. More recently I have been going to a Catholic church and have found this church to be open and accepting of me.

For me it comes down to the fact that this country was founded on the concept of freedom of religion. We need to respect that. There is one big sky above us all, and I believe that the same God put each of us here. Every day I pray for the people I love, and while I might not pray in the same way you do, I believe that God hears our prayers—no matter what religion we practice.

For many years I had been forced to do things I did not believe in, in the name of religion. From the relatively simple matter of the head scarf to the accepted practice of child slavery that is common in many Muslim families in Egypt, I no longer wanted to be forced. I wanted to practice a religion because I chose to, not because a Muslim man slapped me if I didn't.

In addition to the new church, I found that I liked participating in sports. I began to play soccer in 2005 and looked forward to days when I could get out onto the field. I'd never had the opportunity to do that before, and I thought being on a team was great! I loved running and the aggressiveness of soccer. I still had a lot of residual anger and emotion about how life had treated me, and kicking a soccer ball with as much force as I could muster helped dissipate much of that. I had to be careful not to overdo it, though, as I didn't want my RA symptoms to flare up. I played soccer in a community league every year until I was nineteen. Each season I had different teammates and a different coach, and I found it was a great way to get to know lots of people and have a lot of fun at the same time.

Also outside of school I played softball for a time. I can't tell you how wonderful it felt the first time I walked out onto a softball field. I had come a long way from watching the Anaheim Angels play and not understanding anything that was going on, to actually putting on my own glove and being part of a game. But my new parents were part of the coaching staff, and they carried their never-ending fight into the dugout. I had enough of that at home, and their continual sniping at each other ruined the game for me. Fighting aside, I found that I enjoyed watching baseball much more than I liked to play, because there wasn't enough action on the field for me, as compared to soccer. And to be honest, I wasn't that good at either hitting the ball or catching it.

I was on the high school track team for a short time too, but it was too hard on my joints. And the constant practices took up much of my time that otherwise would have been spent doing homework. With the exception of math and English, I had mostly caught up, but it took me much longer than most other students to finish my assignments.

While I was waiting not-so-patiently for the day when I could take my citizenship test, I jumped at the chance during my junior year of high school to join the local police department as a volunteer in their Police Explorer Program. This program is open to young people ages fourteen to twenty-one who have completed at least the eighth grade. Explorers had to go through a rigorous application process and maintain at least a C average in their school studies.

Since the day I'd been rescued, I had wanted a career in law enforcement, and this was a great opportunity for me to get my foot in the door. But while the opportunity was there, it didn't automatically mean that I would be approved for duty. There was a lot to the application process, which was set up to prepare candidates for the similar experience of becoming a police officer.

To start, I had to not only fill out a mountain of paperwork and get fingerprinted, but I also had to meet with a detective who served as an adviser to the program. He, or someone in his department, then did a background check on me. After that I had to meet with a corporal in the department, and after that, the chief of police. That meeting was pretty intimidating for me. I was scared to death. A few short years before, I'd been terrified of anyone involved in law enforcement. Now here I was meeting with the chief of police! But the chief turned out to be a nice man, and he spent most of our time together asking about my personal and education goals. He even went so far as to give me some advice on area colleges. I liked him and couldn't wait to begin.

There were about ten of us in my junior group, and we were one of the first groups to go through the program. I was thrilled on the day that I received my uniform, which consisted of black dress pants, a light blue long-sleeved shirt with black epaulets, and several official patches sewn onto the sleeves. A black tie and belt, and pins on the points of my collar completed the uniform. I was asked to wear my long, dark hair pulled back into a bun, and when I looked at the picture the department had taken for their files, I have to say that I looked every inch the junior officer that I was.

But before I was 100 percent official, I had to pass a test. I had to wait thirty days before I could take it, because the people who set up the program wisely understood that Explorers needed to have some on-the-job experience first. There were roughly thirty questions on the test, and I did fine, even though almost everyone in my group, including me, got the last—and most important—question wrong. The question was something to the effect of, "When should an Explorer use the police radio?" For the life of me I could not think of the answer to that, even though I knew we had gone over it several times. The correct response, by the way, was "Only in an emergency, or when instructed by an officer."

During training the other Explorers and I attended an intense weeklong summer program at the sheriff's academy in Riverside, California. After the other Explorers in my group and I arrived, the kids from different towns were divided into groups, and I ended up being the only person from my local area in my group. Each group stayed in a cabin, and we had to take turns staying up at night to "guard" the cabin and our fellow Explorers. I learned a lot about law enforcement and legal procedures while I was there.

We also spent time doing police drills and running, just as real police officers would. And even though Explorers are unarmed, we got to go through gun training. I learned about different kinds of weapons, how to clean them, and even spent some time target shooting.

The training was rigorous and intense, and several people dropped out. None of us from my town even dared think about that, though. Even though it was a tough week, we knew we'd get much worse from our local supervisors if we didn't complete the course. Plus, we had such a sense of pride that we didn't want to let anyone at our police department down. And we didn't!

After we returned home, the real fun began. I got to work directly with officers when they were on the job. During my shift I might ride with an officer and handle paperwork such as a request to tow a vehicle. Or I might fill out the paperwork during a traffic stop for infractions such as speeding or failing to signal. And I was trained to relay information over the police radio—if an officer instructed me to.

As a police Explorer I often went to public events such as our local cherry festival, bike race, or summer concert series. I would direct traffic, or I might join others to pick up trash, help out in our area's food kitchen (which served meals to the needy), or run errands for officers.

Other times I filed police reports in the records division of the police department, and in the process I got to know almost every officer on the force, and most of the department's support staff too.

Being able to network with those in law enforcement was the best, and I learned a great deal about my chosen career path. It was an invaluable experience, and I stayed until I reached the age limit of twenty-one.

Even then I couldn't get enough. I stayed on another year doing volunteer patrol. This is a program where citizens (mostly retired) drive their own cars around town and call in any suspicious activity. I felt proud whenever I put that VOLUNTEER sign on my car, because I knew I was helping the department.

During my junior year of high school, and while I was adjusting to my new role as a police Explorer, my new mom arranged for a local newspaper reporter to interview me. At the time I was not sure what Patty was thinking or why she set up the interview, but the result was that my story of enslavement and rescue was featured in the local paper. I have to say that as much as I hated the publicity, it helped my social life at school.

Before the article was published, I had a small circle of friends, and a wider group of acquaintances who knew me as the girl with the accent, the girl with the funny name, or the girl in foster care. But once everyone read the story and learned about my past, one after another, people came up to me to talk. I met a lot of kids that way, and some of my teachers even looked at me with an odd expression that might have been admiration. That was my first experience with the power of the press, but it wasn't my last.

That same year I was featured in *Reader's Digest*. I didn't want to do that interview either. But Patty set the interview up and encouraged me to do it. "By sharing your story you will help other people," she said.

I didn't dispute that, but I was a junior in high school. I had missed such a big portion of my childhood that I wanted to savor the lone year that I had left before graduation. I wanted to be a kid. For the first time in a long time, I was happy. I didn't want to be brought back into my past. I needed to focus on the present and on my future, and the interviews kept me from doing that. Yes, I wanted to help others and knew that I would spend the rest of my life doing that. I just wanted to grow up first.

Another consideration was that I was not comfortable with the attention the interviews brought. The first story had been good. It had let people around me know more about me, and because of that I fit in better than I had before. I did several interviews after that, however, and in most of them a privacy line was crossed. Back then I was not comfortable with strangers knowing too much about me. That extra information and the attention it drew only served to again make me different from my classmates. Rather than "Wow, Shyima, you've lived an amazing life," which would have been okay, most of what I heard was, "Oh, poor, poor you." It was depressing.

I didn't want that kind of negative attention and didn't understand why I couldn't be left alone to fit in. Instead of increasing my circle of friends, the later interviews made me even more standoffish than I had been before, and I withdrew into myself.

It wasn't until the next year that I learned that I had gotten paid to do some of the interviews. I had seen a letter from the IRS with my name on it. The letter was about taxes, and I asked Patty and Steve about it. It turned out that since I was a minor, the money was put into an account that they opened in my name, but to which they had access. It took a lot of work to get the tax forms straightened out. In the meantime I continued to put in as many hours as I could in the Explorer program and at work. I had moved on from Godiva and by my senior year of high school was putting in as many as twenty-two hours a week at Kipling.

Kipling was an upscale store that sold handbags, backpacks, and travel accessories. You may have seen some of their products around, as the monkey at the end of the zipper easily identifies them. The store was big on customer service, the products were easy for me to sell because I believed in the quality, and I liked that everything came in awesome colors. I adored my time there and quickly learned my products from top to bottom.

I started at Kipling as a sales associate but over the next few years moved up through the ranks into management. I also embraced any other activity I could find that kept me out of the house and away from the constant fighting there.

CHAPTER THIRTEEN

When I first moved in with Patty and Steve, they told me they didn't want me to date until I was seventeen. It was a reasonable request, but I went ahead and started when I was sixteen. I began dating not as a defiant act against my parents but because I wanted to fit in. What I wanted was to be a regular teenage girl, and my view of that included dating.

Since the day I'd been rescued I had been as far behind socially as I had been academically. While my first two foster homes had helped me catch up with my studies, they'd done little to integrate me into the real world, because I'd been prohibited from talking to boys. Since entering public high school I'd found myself in regular contact with the male species, and at first I felt shy, awkward, and uncomfortable around them. And speaking to a boy? It was beyond me—at first.

Over time I developed a friendship with a nice young man

whom I met at school. He was a sweet, innocent boy who was there for me during the tumultuous times with my family. I wanted to spend time with this person who supported me, and eventually our friendship turned into boyfriend and girlfriend.

This was new, uncharted territory for me. I did not have any close girlfriends, or an older sister whom I could turn to for guidance. Patty was of no help because we had not bonded in such a way that I felt I could talk to her about something like this. Instead I did what I had done over and over again. I watched. I emulated other girls, and eventually my observations helped me feel more comfortable around boys. After all, 50 percent of the people on the planet are men. I needed to know how to interact with them.

The nice boy and I were a couple for about a year but parted ways before our junior prom rolled around. Instead of going to the prom with a "date" date, I went with a boy who was a friend. But I was excited. Prom is a rite of passage for many young people, and it was a milestone that I had once thought I would never achieve. Our theme as a couple was a gangster look. I found a sleeveless floor-length hot pink dress with a scoop neck and had my hair done up in a forties-style chignon. My date had a dark gangster hat with a wide white band along the crown; a dark suit with a short, wide white tie; a boutonniere; and lots of chains hanging from his belt. It was a fun look for a fun night. Our prom was held outdoors in a huge tent, and we got there in my date's brother's big, pimped-out muscle car.

The fact that I had such a great time was a huge testament to how far I had come socially. If I hadn't been able to date, I know I would not have reached as many normal teen landmarks as I did. Keep in mind, however, that my dates were all chaste and innocent. I was far too young for anything more.

My senior year of high school passed with interminable slowness. One highlight was a day when Mark Abend called. After the usual greeting he asked, "Would you by any chance be interested in talking to a group of ICE agents about your time in bondage?"

Would I? "Yes!" I shouted. I didn't even have to think about it. This was a chance for me to use my terrible experience for good. I definitely wanted to help in any way that I could.

On the appointed day Mark picked me up and we both spoke to a group of agents in Southern California. The event was held about an hour away. I wanted to make a difference, but I was so nervous about speaking that I thought I might be sick. Speaking in public is often listed as a person's greatest fear, and I can see why. I wanted to do this, but I was so terrified that I had difficulty swallowing.

Once we began, though, I found my rhythm, and my anxiety eased—somewhat. Mark introduced me, and he began by asking me questions. The initial questions were easy and dealt with the facts of my captivity. Where was I born? When was I sold into slavery? How long was I held?

I answered with short responses at first but soon began expanding my answers. Halfway through I realized that the agents in the audience were listening intently to what I had to say. Once I realized that these people were like Mark, that every person who was listening to my words cared and wanted to be there so they could learn enough to help someone else, my passion for giving people information broke through.

Then the questions from the audience started, and most of them focused on my rescue and integration into life in the United States.

"How could we have made the rescue less stressful for you?" one asked.

"Why did you not trust the law enforcement team who rescued you?" asked another.

On and on and on. The questions came faster and faster. When I explained that I had been brainwashed for years and had thought that anything to do with the police would be far worse than life with my captors, I could see new understanding in the eyes of some of the people in the room. When I explained that my upbringing had led me to believe that my Muslim religion forbade me to speak to a man who was not a member of my immediate family, that an Arabic-speaking woman right there in the patrol car with me rather than on the phone would have made the rescue much less frightening, I saw pens and pencils begin to move on paper.

Speaking was scary for me, but it was empowering, too. And when Mark told me later that the team had made changes in how some of the rescues were going to be executed, based on the information I'd given, I was pumped. How else could I help? I asked. Mark smiled, and he lined up more speaking engagements for me.

. . .

During my senior year I began to have more trouble with my adoptive parents. The case against The Mom and The Dad had been settled before I'd been adopted, and the money I'd gotten from that was supposed to be for me. I had wanted to save the money for my college education, but once my new parents got their hands on the cash, it was soon gone.

At that point in time I did not understand about banks. I received a check from work several times a month, but I always cashed it. No one had explained to me how a bank worked. When the settlement came, a bank account was opened in my name, but my new mom and dad had full access to it.

There were ongoing financial problems within the family, and Steve's car was repossessed. We got it back with my settlement money. When Patty's car broke down, it was repaired with funds from my account. When new furniture arrived, I learned it had been paid for with my settlement.

I was furious. A few times my parents asked if they could use my funds as long as they paid me back, and at first I said yes. But then they must have begun dipping into the account without my knowledge, because after a while the entire $76,137 was gone. I was appalled. That had been *my* money, my future. I had suffered greatly for each cent and deserved every bit.

I did get a car out of it, a car I drive today. But the title was put in my new mom's name because I was underage. I also got a computer, and enough money for a semester or two of community college. But a good deal of the money was spent on who knows what, and I have not yet been paid back any of the money Patty and Steve borrowed.

Money often tears people apart, and this situation definitely drove a wedge between my new family and me. Because they'd been at the sentencing hearing for The Mom and The Dad, they knew how much I had been awarded, and I will always wonder if that was part of their eagerness to adopt me. Unfortunately, I will never know for sure.

I do think that my adoptive dad had genuine warm feelings for me, but from my perspective my new mom behaved more as a big sister than as a mom. I never felt that she had any maternal feelings for me.

No matter the feelings, Steve, Patty, and I had a number of blowout fights over my settlement funds, fights that several times almost caused them to kick me out of the house, and fights that an equal number of times almost made me leave voluntarily. But I stayed because at that point I had nowhere else to go.

I couldn't wait to graduate and move on with my life, but I first had another prom, a math test, and a hospital stay to get through.

For my senior prom I went with another guy friend. I had been dating another nice boy who'd been there for me emotionally. This boy had high morals and ethics, which is something that attracted me to him. But when it came time for our senior prom, he asked my dad if, after the prom, I could spend the night at his house. I believe that he asked in all innocence, but my dad (of course) said no. Then Steve forbade me to see the boy again. That's how I ended up going to my senior prom with another guy who was just a good friend.

This time I wore my favorite color, purple. The dress was satin with a big, puffy knee-length skirt. The icing on the cake for me was my shiny purple shoes and matching nails. Both of my prom dresses were light-years from the hand-me-down clothes I had worn when I'd been in captivity. Each dress made me feel like a princess. A few short years before this, I could never have dreamed that I could wear something so beautiful.

This prom was held in a huge mansion in Palm Springs. The best thing about that prom was the amazing buffet. It seemed as if the tables stretched out forever. Because this was our senior prom and my classmates and I were nearing the end of an era, it was not couple based. Instead bunches of friends grouped together, and I had a blast. We had agreed ahead of time that I would arrive at the prom with my date, but my dad would pick me up after it was over while my date went out to party with his friends.

Prom took up a lot of my attention, but like many other seniors I was also focused on passing all of my finals, including math. Through the years I had done well in PE and in subjects such as social studies and history. In fact, every time I saw a photo from the past, I wanted to learn more about it. My natural curiosity helped me there, but not in English and math. Those two subjects continued to be my downfall.

Through my daily use of the English language and the remedial

English classes that I took, I was getting by in that subject, but I often received near-failing grades in math. My lack of knowledge in this subject is a sad fact of my time in bondage. When I should have been learning my numbers—and learning how to add and subtract them—I was instead cleaning toilets and washing my captors' clothes.

After taking my final exams, I was fairly certain I had passed all of them, with the exception of math. That subject I wasn't sure about. Even though, emotionally, I was done with school and the last thing I wanted was to have to sit through a summer math course, I knew I would take the class—and pass it—if I needed to.

It was a stressful time for me because if I didn't pass the test, I would not get to graduate. If I didn't graduate, I could not go to college or become a police officer or ICE agent. A high school diploma was my gateway to the life I wanted to live, and graduation was a must.

Another reason graduation was important to me was because I had felt helpless for many years because I'd not been able to communicate with anyone. I'd also spent many years in a position where I'd had no options. I never wanted to be in either of those places again. Ever. Early on after my rescue I realized that paying attention to my studies was my best option. I had tried my best. But had I succeeded?

I made it a point to stay positive while I waited for my test results, but it was hard. A great deal rode on the result of that math test. By this time the rest of the seniors and I were winding up our classes. I worked as much as I could and waited to hear if I would graduate. I couldn't focus on much of anything, so between work shifts I wandered around the house and flipped from channel to channel on television. On the chance that I had passed, I took some of the money that I had earned and paid for my class ring and my cap and gown. When my new dad bought a class sweater for me, I hoped I would be able to wear it with the pride of a high school graduate.

Less than a week before the graduation ceremony a letter came for me from the school. Somehow I knew that whatever news the letter held would determine my future. With nervous anticipation I opened the letter and held my breath as I read the words on the page. I almost couldn't believe it. I had passed. I had *passed*! I released the tension I didn't know I had been holding and let out a whoop of joy. I was a high school graduate, and I was going to get to walk down the aisle with my classmates, cross the stage, and pick up my diploma.

This was such a huge achievement for me, for less than six years before, I hadn't understood English. I hadn't known my letters or what a mall was. I had never been to a doctor or a dentist, had had no social skills, and had mistrusted virtually everyone around me. But now, now I was a high school graduate, and no matter what happened in the future, no one could take that away from me. I was so happy that I hugged the letter to me and cried.

I know many other people would have gotten on the phone right away to share the news, but I didn't. For years I'd had nothing that was my own, but this was *my* triumph—and I didn't want to share it. At least not right away. I savored my success for the rest of the day, and then I called everyone.

Our senior class party was held a day or so later on a party boat off the coast. I had wanted to attend this event knowing that I was going to be a graduate, and I did! I had a great time with my friends, and we were thrilled about having an open door to our future, and to the world around us.

My joy was not to last long, however, because the next day I became desperately ill. In June of almost every year I come down with a bad flu-type illness, and this year was no exception. Plus, the night air, wind, and chill of being on the boat had hastened this year's illness along. Within hours I found myself in a hospital bed with a high fever and a painful sore throat. Because of my rheumatoid arthritis, my immune system was not strong, and illnesses like this could quickly become life threatening if they were not monitored.

I was miserable. On top of being sick, I had wanted to attend my graduation ceremony and now it didn't look as if I were going to be able to do that. I was sad and emotionally drained as I lay in my hospital bed. In fact, I was beyond disappointed that I might miss the pomp and circumstance of my big day. Why did this have to happen to me now? I had worked hard. Why could I not enjoy the celebration with everyone else? A tear slipped down my cheek, but I did not give in to despair. I knew I had to stay mentally positive if I were to beat this illness in time for my graduation ceremony.

And I did. With fluids, antibiotics, positive thoughts, the

prayers of friends—and rest—I improved, and was released from the hospital on June 5, 2008, the day before my class graduated from high school.

Even though I had been released from the hospital, I was so stiff and weak that I could not walk any kind of distance. Walking across my room was enough to send me to my knees, and I knew there was no possible way that I could walk the length of an entire auditorium. Staff at my school knew it too.

At the last minute Mr. Steele, my math teacher, suggested that he push me into the auditorium and across the stage in a wheelchair. I was extremely grateful for his idea. I liked Mr. Steele a lot as a teacher, and if not for his kind patience and dedication toward me, I would not have been graduating. It was a good kind of karma that he was the one to push me toward victory.

While my friends went out to celebrate after the ceremony, I went home. The medication for my illness, combined with the meds for my RA, had wiped me out. In fact, I don't remember much about my graduation, just bits and pieces here and there. But I recall enough, and I will hold on to those memories for the rest of my life. In spite of my illness, it was a great, great day.

After graduation I wanted to join the air force, but my new family discouraged me from doing so. Patty said, "Why would you want to do that? You wouldn't be able to handle any of the instruction. Besides, people who want to do stuff like that really put their hearts into it."

Her words broke my heart. I didn't understand why she could not be supportive of my goals and interests. Even if she'd had reservations about my ability to succeed in that kind of environment, I wish she had encouraged me to try. Steve almost always followed his wife's lead on things, and on this he was not much more supportive than she was.

I was hurt by their belief that I was not serious about the air force or that I didn't have enough heart to care about the job I might do there. I knew I had to obtain citizenship first, and I was waiting until the day when I could apply for that. I, more than anyone else, knew my health might prevent me from being accepted into the air force, but I would rather have had the medical people there give me that news than have my parents shoot my dream to the ground. Without the support from my family, my dream of entering the air force became tainted for me and I never pursued it.

Instead I worked throughout that next summer, and in the fall I began attending community college. I took general, required classes to start with, as well as my usual remedial English class. I was still working at Kipling—and going out to dinner, movies, and parties several evenings a week with my friends.

In essence I went home only to sleep, shower, and change clothes. That was by design because my tenuous relationship with my adoptive mom was unraveling. A big part of the problem was that I felt that Patty wanted to have control over me. I was paying my family rent to stay in my room, and I paid their entire electric bill every month. Because of that I felt I should be able to come and go as I pleased. And it wasn't as if I were having loud parties there or didn't do my share of household chores. I never had friends over, always took care of my clothes, kept my room clean, and did many other household tasks.

My relationship with Patty deteriorated to the point where I often slept either at my friend Amber's house or at my friend Karla's. I had met Karla Pachacki my first day at Kipling. We'd been the two newbies, and we'd quickly bonded. Karla made my shifts there a lot of fun, and when I'd introduced Karla to Amber, the three of us had become great friends.

At first I was hesitant to tell either Karla or Amber about my past, but over time my trust in them developed and I began to share my story. I am glad that I did, because I needed their support in my struggles with my new family. And to support me as I needed to be, my new friends needed to understand my past.

One day in the middle of yet another argument, Patty said, "You are a bad influence on my kids." I had no idea what she was talking about, but her words made me realize that I was fighting a losing battle. With some people there is always tension, always conflict, and she was that kind of person. She was so unsupportive of me that I felt that she would always try to prevent any dream I had from becoming a reality. I'd had enough, and I began to look for my own place.

Apartment hunting was both fun and a challenge. It was time consuming and slow, too. By the time I had researched a complex, toured the unit, met with the supervisor, filled out the application, and waited for it to be processed, someone else had already rented the place. This happened several times before Amber and her mother, Teresa, said, "Why don't you move in with us?"

It made perfect sense. During the several years that I had known Amber, Teresa had become like a second mom to me. She always had a big smile on her face and was so giving that I felt both loved and supported by her. Plus, they had the perfect setup for me—a pool house. This space gave me the room I needed for my things— and I had a lot of stuff! I think after my years in bondage, during which I had nothing, I went overboard when I first began to earn a paycheck. I bought a lot of clothes and makeup, and still do. In a strange way, having "stuff" makes me feel secure. Someday I will probably get past that, but when I moved into Amber and Teresa's, having many things of my own comforted me.

The pool house gave me privacy, but at the same time I knew I was fully welcome in their home anytime I wanted. If I needed a midnight snack, all I had to do was walk across the patio and into the kitchen. In fact, Amber and Teresa treated me more like family than either my biological or adoptive families had.

Teresa's mom and dad also lived in the house, so there were several generations for me to bond with. I adored each member of that family and every minute I spent with them. But I was not completely happy. The biggest drawback of leaving my adoptive home in the way that I had was that I now had limited access to my younger brother and sisters. I both loved and missed them.

Karla was of special help to me during this time. In the course of a number of conversations over many months, she helped open my eyes to the many issues with my adoptive family.

Karla then helped me get rid of a lot of my anger toward my new parents by helping me see them as individuals, and as a couple. Karla was a few years older, but I was still at the age when it was hard for me to see parental figures as people rather than as a mom or a dad. Once I made that leap, many things about their relationship with each other became clear. I felt as if they had used me to facilitate their dysfunction. Karla encouraged me to close the bank account Patty and Steve had access to. Once that was done, I felt far less vulnerable where my adoptive parents were concerned.

With my new place and my new support team, I began to thrive. The pool house was a wonderful transition for me, and I stayed there for the better part of seven months. It takes true friends to open their home to another person, and Amber and Teresa never hesitated when I needed a place to stay. I will never forget that. They are still my chosen family.

I eventually began to look at apartment complexes again, and this time I found a nice one-bedroom unit. It was small, but I had fun decorating the place. I found a tall, trendy, dark brown dining set and a matching sectional couch, then added a queen mattress and pad, and a dresser. I painted the bathroom purple and didn't mind that there wasn't enough room in the closets or dresser for my clothes.

By this time I had two closets full of clothes. And makeup.

I had a lot of that, too. But the difference between many other young women and me is that I looked at my two closets of clothes and thought that I was living in the lap of luxury. Many people would see the modest place I lived in and my full closets and not realize what a wonderful gift it was.

After I moved in, I had clothes everywhere. But you know what? They were *my* clothes in *my* apartment. I loved that place, loved setting my own budget and arranging the furniture where I wanted it to be. I found I liked cooking for myself too—cooking what I wanted when I wanted how I wanted. For much of my life I'd had no control over anything. Now I could control almost everything, and I reveled in that change.

I was fortunate to have good neighbors around me. We looked out for one another, and there was a sense of community that is hard to find in most apartment complexes. For maybe the first time since I'd been taken from my family, I was truly happy. I'd had bits of happiness before. Two of my happiest moments had been when The Mom and The Dad had been handcuffed and when I'd graduated from high school. But sustained happiness had been hard for me to find. Plus, when I was younger I'd never envisioned that I could have this much independence or have such a nice place of my own. This little apartment was, for me, a dream come true.

By this time I rarely thought of my biological family, or where life might have taken me if I had stayed with them. Even now I was traumatized enough by my separation from my family, and my ensuing years with The Mom and The Dad, that my biological family was often too painful to think about. My sisters were strong women, and on the rare occasion when I did think of them, I hoped they had better lives than that of my mother. The biological ties were there, though, and I hoped that someday, when I was ready, we could reconnect.

During this time I was both working and paying my way through college. When I first applied for grants and student loans, I found that as long as I was under the age of twenty-four, my applications were dependent on the income of my parents. If I had not been adopted, I would have qualified for money for school from many different sources. But since I had been adopted, my new mom and dad's income came into play. Unfortunately, Steve made an adequate amount of money, but it was spent as fast as he made it. The result was that they did not have funds for my education, or the credit to obtain the funds.

I gritted my teeth as I thought about the tens of thousands of lost dollars from my settlement. But I bit the bullet and paid my own way. I liked college, but it wasn't working out as I had hoped. The looser structure made it harder for me to achieve, and the busy professors did not have as much time to spend with me as my high school teachers had. The result: I dropped out.

Normally I make it a point to finish everything that I start. It is a matter of pride for me, a matter of honor. My friends encouraged me to stay in class, but the tougher subject matter and faster pace of the classes were too frustrating for me at that time in my life. I do plan to continue my education someday, under different circumstances, so I look at this as a temporary stop.

While I was terribly disappointed, I knew that the lack of a college degree would not affect my ultimate goal of becoming an ICE agent. Being a college grad would help, I knew, but it was not a requirement. I often think how important early education is for young children and wish I'd had that opportunity. I had come a long way, had made more than amazing strides, but in many areas of education I had a long way to go. Another college may have been better equipped to handle my special needs. Or not. I encourage anyone who is reading this to go as far as they can in school, even if it means significant sacrifice. In the long run it will be worth it.

Instead of putting my efforts into school, I now concentrated on becoming a great employee. Being employed validated me in many ways. After many years of verbal abuse when I was in bondage, of being called "stupid girl," I had a huge need to prove to myself and to others that I had value. My job and recent promotion did just that. I was now a supervisor and felt proud to be in a managerial position. I rose to my new responsibilities and some days wanted to pinch myself to be sure all this good fortune truly was mine.

CHAPTER FOURTEEN

Since I had moved out, life had not gotten any better for my adoptive family, and my new mom and dad divorced. Because Steve did not have any place to go, he moved in with me. Many of my friends wondered why I allowed this, but I felt that much of the trouble in the family, including the financial issues that had caused the draining of my settlement account, started with Patty, not Steve.

After several months of sleeping on my couch (and not paying rent) Steve got on his feet enough that he could get a place of his own. Not that I wish for the demise of any marriage, but I think he is a better person when he is apart from Patty. Some people are just not good together.

Since the divorce I have not seen much of my adoptive mom, but Steve is trying. He has made mistakes with each of his children, and will probably make more, but I give him credit for his efforts. Besides, we are all human, and I do believe that his intentions are good. We don't have the best of relationships yet, but we are working toward that. I hope that someday we will be as close as we should be.

The real tragedy in the divorce is that I now do not have any contact with my adoptive brother and sisters. I hope that when my new siblings become legal adults, we can pick up where we left off, because I love them a great deal. The lack of contact is especially hard for me because this is the second set of younger siblings that I have lost in about fifteen years. Add to that the two sets of foster siblings that I lost. If I think about it too much, it tears my heart apart.

The good news was that I was busy with work and my friends, so when Steve was living with me, I didn't see him that often. Even better, I was doing some speaking that occasionally sent me out of state.

Through Mark, I continued to speak to audiences about my time in captivity. All told I must have stood in front of several dozen audiences. Maybe, just maybe, some other slave would be rescued as a result of my letting people know what to look for. Or someone else might not be as traumatized as I'd been during the rescue. I was excited to spread this kind of awareness, even though the nervous, sickly feeling that I had before every speaking engagement never went away.

Steve came with me to a few of the events, and I was glad

that he could see firsthand the difference I was making, as well as learn more about my past. I had never been forthcoming about the details of my ordeal in slavery. Usually I told people the basic facts and then asked them to Google me. I had not spoken publicly before the sentencing hearing for The Mom and The Dad but had spoken to the press half a dozen times or more since then. By now there were enough articles about me out there that people could get a good feel for what had happened. Reliving the details over and over with new friends was hard for me, and referring someone to a Google search kept me from emotional upheaval every time I met someone new.

I was not sure how much my adoptive parents had been told about my past. Sure, they knew my biological parents had sold me into slavery. They knew many of the facts, since I had lived with them while the case against The Mom and The Dad had been going on. But I do not think they had been told many of the details, how I'd been forbidden to use the family's bathroom because I was too dirty, that I'd had to wash my clothes in a bucket, that I'd not been allowed medical attention when I was sick, that I'd born the brunt of anger for every member of the family in the form of stinging slaps.

I could see the pained expression on Steve's face as one detail after another spilled out. But I could also see brains whirring and clicking as the law enforcement officials in my audiences developed new ideas and protocols that would make future rescues and integrations safer and smoother.

Local speaking events gave way to larger events out of state, and I flew to Houston, Dallas, North Carolina, Georgia, Saint Paul, Saint Louis, and many other cities and states. Since my arrival in the United States, before these trips I had flown only twice—to my foster home in central California and back. It was stunning to realize that the first time I stepped aboard a plane on the way to a speaking engagement was the first time I had ever flown of my own free will. I have to say—it felt great! Even better was the knowledge that I could make a positive difference.

Sometimes Mark came with me, but other times I went alone. I was surprised that so many people were interested to hear my perspective and feelings about my rescue and its aftermath. But I was gratified and excited. The more people I could reach, the better chance we had of ending the hateful practice of human trafficking.

Some of the speaking engagements paid me a small fee, while others paid only my expenses. While the fees were nice, I never turned an event down because of the lack of payment. If I could get the time off work and if I was healthy enough to do so, I went. In addition to the events, I enjoyed the travel. I liked meeting new people and learning firsthand what the many different cities were like. But the biggest thrill for me was the realization that I was doing any traveling. During my time in captivity not once had I ever thought my negative experience could be put to such great use.

At some of the conferences I got to see Andrew and Robert, my lawyers who'd worked diligently to prepare my case against The Mom and The Dad. It was great to keep in touch with them, especially because I kept in touch with only a few people from my past. I was shocked to realize that with the exception of a very few, I had known for only a few short years the people who were in my life now.

In Saint Louis I spoke to hundreds of lawyers from across the country, and all I could think was what a positive impact they could make for people like me, people who had been held against their will. A lot of their questions showed their need to recognize the different forms of human trafficking. One form of human trafficking involves the recruitment, transportation, transfer, harboring, or receipt of people though threat, force, coercion, abduction, fraud, deception, or the abuse of power.

The second form of human trafficking is slavery in the historical sense, where a person is stripped of all rights and is trafficked, "owned," or controlled by others. For example, I was trafficked illegally into the United States, but the work I was forced to do, the conditions in which I lived, my lack of pay, and my captors' control over my movements resulted in my slavery.

I loved this Saint Louis group and their intelligent questions.

In Glynco, Georgia (halfway between Savannah, Georgia, and Jacksonville, Florida), I spoke to a large group of ICE agents at the Federal Law Enforcement Training Center. These people had such great questions that I knew each of them was as passionate about his or her job as Mark was. Government officials often get a bad reputation, but I have to say that the people who are trying to stop the practice of human trafficking are the best.

By this time I had realized that law enforcement officers often did not understand the victim's point of view. Police officers and ICE agents were focused on upholding the law and getting their man (or woman), which meant the victim often got lost. My role was to show them how to be more understanding. To do this I told them of other victims I had met who were depressed and without hope because no one believed in them. I mentioned how these compassionate law enforcement officers had an opportunity to be that person who cared, just as for years Mark Abend was the one constant person in my life who cared about me. I hope they took my words to heart, because the difference they can make to the victim can be everything.

Early on in my travels I had been concerned that the flying, hotel rooms, and strange food would bother my arthritis. But I needn't have worried. I was holding up well as long as I didn't get too tired, and as long as I didn't allow myself to get too cold. A luxury I usually allow myself pretty much every day are high heels. I am barely five feet tall, so I love heels. When my RA flares, however, I am reduced to wearing flats, and I always brought a pair with me when I traveled, just in case. I usually wear warmer clothes during a flare than might otherwise be warranted, so I made sure I packed for that, too. I can't take a soothing hot bath when traveling on a plane, but a soft, warm sweater is the next-best thing.

At some point a woman who worked for the Associated Press

came to do an interview with me. At the end of it she told me she was going to Egypt. "Maybe," she said, "I can find your family and get them to talk with you."

It had been several years since I had last spoken to any of them. After the hurt I had experienced when I'd realized that members of my family were ready to testify against me—and for The Mom and The Dad if their case ever went to trial—I hadn't wanted anything to do with them. But they *were* my family. I held out a tiny bit of hope that we could be friendly, that my family still wanted me.

Maintaining family ties is a theme of many who are rescued out of slavery. Many of us can't go back to our families (there are as many reasons for this as there are people who are rescued), but it is a natural human emotion to want your family to want you. I was no different.

I did not hold out much hope that the woman who spoke to me would find my family, or even try, but to my amazement she did both. On a day when I was speaking in yet another city, I was alone in my hotel room when my phone rang. I was astonished to find two of my sisters and my mother on the other end of the line. One sister was the one who had lived with my grandparents, and the other was the "nice" twin. Their big news was that my father had died. One of my sisters told me, and when I heard her words, I didn't know what to think or what emotion to feel.

My entire past came back in a rushing whoosh, and I was saddened that I'd never gotten to know my dad. Almost every interaction I'd had with him had shown him to be angry and domineering, but had he lived longer, I might eventually have taken the opportunity to try to discover a different side to him. Now that chance was gone forever.

To make the conversation even more difficult, my mother said, "His last wish was to see you and talk to you. He wanted to ask you to forgive him; he was so very sorry."

I was at a loss for words. What could I say to that, knowing what had happened to me because of him?

Then my mother added, "I'm not doing so well either. I wish I could see you once more."

This had my thoughts and emotions jumping all over the place. From one second to the next I was thinking and feeling entirely different things. I had not expected either the news about my dad or what I was now feeling. Eventually I realized that while I did want to see my mom, I wanted the life I had in California much more. I was afraid that if I saw any of my relatives in Egypt, I would be dragged into a family drama that I was not equipped to deal with. I tried to explain that to my mother, but I do not think she understood.

Part of that was because my Arabic was pretty rusty by that time, and my mother spoke no English. We spoke through a translator who was in Egypt with my family, but I know that a lot of the details from both sides of the conversation got lost. Language is of huge importance to communication. Our lack of ability to communicate through words was another huge sign of the wedge that had been driven between my family after I had been sold into slavery.

When my sisters got back on the line, one said that three of my brothers had joined the Egyptian army. Then she mentioned that another sister had named one of her babies after me. And I found out that my sister who'd stolen, the one whose actions had taken me away from my family in the first place, had a baby too.

After we hung up, my fragile feelings got the best of me, and I lay on the bed and began to cry hard enough that I thought I'd never stop. I was devastated that I had not gotten to see my dad before he'd died. I had dozens of questions for him that would now never be answered. Why had he not fought for me? How could he have slapped me as often as he had if he'd loved me? Why had he not welcomed me back into my family after I'd been rescued? Why had my siblings gotten to grow up in the family home, as meager and dysfunctional as it was, while I'd been sold like a piece of furniture? Why?

During the coming weeks and months I thought a lot about the phone conversation with my mother and sisters, and I knew that if I truly wanted to go to Egypt to see my family, I could probably find a way. I realized, however, that I didn't want to go. Not then. I was not ready. I had let a lot of my anger go, but there was enough left that was still simmering inside me that I did not feel a meeting would be a good thing right then.

The main reason for my decision was that even though these people were my biological family, they were no longer my real family. I had made a new family with my friends Amber, Teresa, and Karla, and even with Mark and my adoptive dad. These were the people who had loved and supported me for years, and through their actions they had earned the right to be called family. That was not the case with my biological parents and siblings.

Another factor was that I did not know my biological family anymore. Because of the circumstances of my life, my family in Egypt and I no longer had the same points of reference, the same religion, or the same viewpoints. We had nothing in common, and if truth be told, I didn't even remember most of them.

I didn't rule out going to Egypt at some point in the future, though. I wasn't sure if my mother's claim of poor health was real or not, and I knew that if it was, I might miss my opportunity to see her again. If that happened, I'd just have to accept it. I knew that I had gathered together all the facts, feelings, and emotions, and I made the best choice for me.

I do think about my family whenever I hear of all the unrest that is happening in Egypt now. I do know that someday I would like to show my brothers and sisters that there is more to the world than what they have experienced. I'd like to show them that a better life awaits them, even if it is in another country. But the reality is that some days I am more open to this idea than others. What I can say for sure is that if the opportunity for us to meet presents itself in the future, I will think about it.

I was glad the woman I had met had taken the time to track down my family, and I was even okay with the fact that it ended up as a story that was broadcast across the Internet. I was grateful for the chance to speak with them. But I knew too that I needed time before I took another step toward my biological family. Actually, I might need a long, long time.

CHAPTER FIFTEEN

One of the lingering effects from my time in captivity was my lack of trust—of both people and situations. It takes me a long time to warm up to someone, even on a casual level. Mark was patient with me in the early days after my rescue. Even before we could communicate directly, when we were talking through a translator, Mark kept on trying to let me know that he was safe, that he was someone I could always trust and count on. He did that by speaking to me not as a victim but as a person. He asked over and over how I was doing, how I liked to spend my time, what I would like for myself for the future.

I didn't realize it then, but these are questions that friends ask each other. Since that time, any new person I meet has to take it almost as slowly as Mark did with me ten years ago. Because my world was upside down then, and because my childhood was not a childhood, I relate to new people in my life differently than many other people do.

I have realized that I must gain trust in people through situations before I can trust them as people. For example, if the situation is that it is busy at a store where I work and an employee is having a meltdown, that employee is not someone I will be able to trust in the future. In another situation, if I am riding in a car with someone and we have a flat, if that person wants my trust, he or she had better act with calm action rather than with angry words.

Once I have seen people act honorably in trying situations, I might then let them in on a more personal level. But if my new friend has told me she is going to meet me at eight o'clock, she had better be there at eight. If she isn't, I will lose trust in her. If an employee at my store is responsible for ordering supplies, he had better do his job and order the supplies. If not, I will not feel that I can trust him.

I do not mean to sound rigid, but to some extent we are a product of our environment. My lack of trust is only one thing that being held in captivity did to me. However, if I find I can trust you to do what you say you are going to, then we might even become friends. This way of thinking was helpful to me in all areas of my life, but especially when it came to dating.

When I first started going out with boys, if my date slipped up even once, that was it for him. Good-bye, you're gone. I feel sorry for some of those boys now, for they were kids, and kids make mistakes. I feel bad for me, too, because I probably pushed some good people out of my life way too soon. But I could not take the chance. I had been beaten up, threatened, ordered around, and given so many broken promises by the men in my life that if the boy I dated wasn't rock solid, I wanted nothing to do with him.

Of course, many of the women in my life had not treated me well either. My mother had sold me into slavery, and my two foster moms and my adoptive mother had each been difficult in their own ways. I still believe in the goodness of people. I think it was bad luck that in my early years I was surrounded by adults who were quite into themselves. The unfortunate result was that there was nothing left over for them to give to others.

It took me a long time to learn how to separate the good people around me from the bad. Was a male teacher abusive like my biological dad? Or was he a stand-up, honest guy? I'd had much of the former and little of the latter, and it was not easy for me to figure out which was which. But I had to.

For someone else, someone who has had long-standing relationships with people they have known, loved, and trusted all their life, surrounding themselves with honorable, trustworthy people might not be such a big deal. But I'd had none of those kinds of relationships, which is why letting only the right kind of people into my life was much more of a survival tactic for me than for others.

I look back to my time in captivity, and to the times when I took the twins to the park across the street and to the nearby pool.

Those visits offered me the chance to observe many different kinds of people, to see how the way they walked affected their tone of voice, to view how they positioned their body next to other people and what that did to their facial expressions. I studied people so intently then that I probably got the equivalent of a college degree in body language. Those visits provided me with a foundation on which to base my current relationships.

Eventually I got to where I could tell pretty quickly if a girlfriend was in my life because we had a lot in common or if she wanted to be around me because my picture had been in the newspaper. I knew right away if a boy thought I was a pushover because my English was not perfect, or if he wanted to take advantage of my generosity. I figured a lot of that out when I was in high school, and have refined the process since.

After dating a boy for a number of months, I was proud of myself when I broke up with him because I didn't like us together. I liked him fine, and I liked me. But together we were not a good fit. That was a huge revelation for me. That was the first time I stopped being around a boy because of how *he* was, rather than for how he compared to the men in my past.

Now I can pick up a vibe from a person that lets me know right away whether this is a good person or someone who might hurt me in the end. This ability came in especially handy when I saw a man who worked at a store in the same mall where I worked. This guy was independent, cute, smart, and sexy, and he had a great vibe about him. Even without knowing him I felt he was safe.

He looked to be several years older than I was and was a store manager, which let me know that his bosses thought he was a responsible person.

Through an odd coincidence I realized the man's name was Daniel Uquidez and that I knew his brother, who worked at the mall too. The mall was large, but many of the employees of the different stores were friendly with one another, so it was fairly easy for me to meet Daniel. After that I regularly found excuses to walk by his store and wave, or to stop in with a friend who wanted to buy something. When I'd see him in the courtyard, or on the way to or from the parking lot, we'd talk. I loved making him smile.

I liked the fact that I had been introduced to Daniel in a professional setting. To him, I was the girl who worked in a nearby store. This was not the way most other people met or knew of me. Usually I was "the girl who used to be a slave" or "the girl who is always in the newspaper." I was much more than that, and those old identities rubbed me the wrong way. I was glad that Daniel knew me first as someone else, before he discovered that older part of me.

Our friendship developed slowly, and I liked that, too. The slow pace gave me time to think whether or not this was someone I wanted to spend more time with, or if I should keep our relationship light, friendly, and professional.

After I met Daniel, I switched jobs and began working again at Godiva. This was late in 2010. I worked there only for a few months before that store closed and I found myself as a sales associate at Versace. This was during a time when jobs were hard to come by, and I felt fortunate to get the job, but I especially liked that I was still working at the mall where I could see Daniel regularly during the day. Additionally, after I learned the Versace product line, I found that I believed fully in it, which made it easy for me to generate sales.

The days and weeks went by during which I learned more about Daniel. He was from a large, close Catholic family, and from casual conversation we seemed to have a lot of the same thoughts and feelings about the important things in life. We even both have asthma.

But even with that, if Daniel had pushed me and asked me out right away, I might have felt too uncomfortable to agree. But he waited until we had known each other for a number of months, and when he did ask, I gave him a resounding yes.

Daniel later told me he had been working up the courage to ask me out for some time. He saw me as a strong, independent woman, and he had grown up with many of those in his family. I am glad that he asked me out because he respected me. I think if more relationships began this way, there would be much less fighting and fewer divorces.

Daniel knew how much I loved baseball, and in particular the Anaheim Angels, so he took me to a home game for our first date. Later I learned that he didn't even like baseball that much, but it was important to him that we do something I liked. That was when I knew he was a keeper.

In the days following the game, we went to three movies in three days. After that we were pretty much inseparable. He knows how peaceful and healing I find the beach, and we went there a lot, even though we do not have a beach anywhere close to where we live. Huntington Beach is several hours away in good traffic, but we like it because it is clean and nice, and not too crowded. Also, the stores and restaurants near there stay open later than at some of the other beaches. We also went to Santa Monica some nights to hear the bands play along the water. Dancing and eating at restaurants that were new to us were activities we often did closer to home. We even went to Disneyland.

Since the day when I'd gone to Disneyland with The Mom and The Dad and the twins, I had been there several times. I had gone with my foster families, and the first time I went after being rescued, it was weird. I had flashes of standing to the side with the boys' backpacks while they enjoyed the rides. But I had no thoughts like that with Daniel. In a reminder of how far I had come, life felt so natural with Daniel that I was able to let the bad things that had happened to me stay in my past.

There was another way that Daniel was different from other boys I had dated—in how we fought. Like many other couples we had several stupid fights. The fights were so stupid, in fact, that I have forgotten what they were about. When we argued the first time, my initial reaction was to think, *He's just another of those guys. Good-bye!* But I thought that for only a fleeting instant with Daniel, because my second reaction was to think, *He's not like the Muslim men who mistreated me.* And he wasn't.

Through those fights I realized that I not only liked Daniel, but I liked him with me, and I liked me with him. We were a good fit.

From Daniel, to Amber, Teresa, Karla, and PaNou Thao (another amazing woman I met at work who became a dear friend), by the time I was twenty-one, I had surrounded myself with strong, reliable, responsible, caring, fun friends. These people had become my inner circle, and I felt like a treasured member of each of their families when I spent Christmas, Thanksgiving, and Easter holidays with them. Some holidays I had a great many invitations and had to split the day into three or four parts just so I could see everyone. I have come to feel that I am the luckiest girl in the world to have each of these people in my life. Together my friends are far better than a biological family because my friends are here because they want to be. With some bio families they are family only because they have to be.

All of my friends have such a positive attitude about life that I love to be around them. I did not initially seek out people with these qualities, but early on I must have known subconsciously that I needed them.

During my time in bondage, and after, I had a lot of time to think about people. I realized that if you are around bad, negative people, that is what you become. The Mom and The Dad both felt entitled. They thought they were better than everyone else, and because of that they thought they must deserve better treatment. Their kids felt the same way. The Mom and the Dad also had bad tempers, as did their children. And they had the childish reaction to slap someone if they became angry. Who wants to be around negative people like that?

In high school I saw people pulled downward by "friends" who were always in trouble. I saw people become the company they kept and lose out on many good opportunities that came their way because of it, such as college and good-paying jobs. But I saw the other end of the spectrum too. I saw the respect that Mark and his coworkers had for one another, and I saw the friendships that developed out of that respect. My own friends showed me through their actions over a long period of time that they were loyal and trustworthy. We didn't always agree, but when we disagreed, we did it respectfully.

Now I know that if I want to live and work in a fabulous environment, if I want to continue to learn and grow in life to become a better person, I have to surround myself with positive people who support me in my goals.

I know many people who are full of shades of gray. These people can deliberate and debate a decision for weeks and never move forward. Those people walk between the lines of good and bad and never find either. That is not me. I am a black-and-white person who has found that most often there are only two courses of direction. Right and wrong. Good and bad. When you think about it, the good and right direction is always pretty clear. That good and right way, however, is not always the easy way, and that is the downfall of many people.

After I came to the United States, I figured out that The Mom and The Dad knew it was not right that I was in their household in the capacity that I was. They knew, because I was forbidden to answer the door or the phone. When non-Muslim guests came over, I had to hide in the pantry. The right and good thing would have been to send me back to my family, or to turn me over to social services. But they made the selfish choice to keep me there, hidden away, and that was wrong.

Their wrong choice not only sent them to prison, but their children were deported back to Egypt. Their wrong choice broke up their family unit. Through Mark and through newspaper reports, I heard that The Mom was deported after her prison term was completed in 2008. I heard too that she has another young girl in her home in Egypt who does not go to school, and who is rarely seen outside. The practice of child slavery is illegal in Egypt, but because it is widely accepted, The Mom must not feel that she is at any risk of legal action for it there.

Mark told me that somewhere along the way The Mom and The Dad divorced, but apparently it was dangerous for The Dad to go back to Egypt. Whatever he had done there must have been quite bad. Another wrong choice. He remarried here in the United States to a US citizen. This was soon after his divorce and his release from prison in 2009. If The Dad is married to a United

States citizen and stays out of trouble here, he can remain on US soil. Sometime after The Dad's remarriage, an immigration judge ruled that The Dad was deportable, but then the judge said he did not have to leave. After the judge's ruling, Immigration and Customs Enforcement released The Dad from their custody but put him under an order of supervision, which means he has to check in with them regularly.

I have also learned through Mark and my legal team that as soon as he could, The Dad sold the house that I lived in when I was being held captive. I was told he may have done that so he would not have to give me the house. His lawyers must have thought that was a possible outcome of any future trial or settlement hearing, because he sold the house in record time. I am sure that particular wrong choice will come back to bite him somewhere down the line too.

Each of these decisions that The Dad made moved not just him but his entire family toward the line of disintegration. He could easily have been a kinder man, a more compassionate man who made good choices and lived an honest life. But he wasn't. And he didn't. I knew I did not want to be around anyone who made decisions as he did. That's why everyone who is now allowed into my life must choose right and good. In the long run it is the easiest choice.

I have been asked several times if I have any fear because The Dad is still in the United States. My answer is no. I have absolutely no desire to ever lay eyes on that man again, and I imagine he wants to put his conviction here behind him and just live his life.

Plus, I am no longer the weak child who lived in his home. I am a strong woman now, and he holds no threat for me. And because he has served his time for what he did to me, I hold no threat to him. The United States, I have found, is a big country. While I'd rather he not be here, there is room for us both.

CHAPTER SIXTEEN

The year 2011 was special for me. This was the year when I could finally become a citizen of the United States of America. The process, I learned, is called naturalization.

Becoming a citizen of the United States takes a lot of paperwork. I first had to fill out a ten-page application that included questions about my place of residence, education, employment, any marriages I might have had, travel outside the United States, and organizations I was affiliated with. Then there were questions about my moral character, and whether I drank, gambled, or used drugs. There was even a place for me to change my name, if I wanted to. I had already done that when I'd been adopted and didn't feel the need to do it again, so I left that space blank.

The most important questions, though, were those that asked if I supported our Constitution and form of government in the United States. I had to check off boxes that said that I not only

understood the full Oath of Allegiance to the United States of
America, but that I was willing to make it. Yes, I absolutely did
and was. The oath says:

> I hereby declare, on oath, that I absolutely and
> entirely renounce and abjure all allegiance and
> fidelity to any foreign prince, potentate, state or
> sovereignty, of whom or which I have heretofore
> been a subject or citizen; that I will support and
> defend the Constitution and laws of the United
> States of America against all enemies, foreign and
> domestic; that I will bear true faith and allegiance
> to the same; that I will bear arms on behalf of the
> United States when required by the law; that I will
> perform noncombatant service in the armed forces
> of the United States when required by the law;
> that I will perform work of national importance
> under civilian direction when required by the law;
> and that I take this obligation freely without any
> mental reservation or purpose of evasion; so help
> me God.

I couldn't wait to stand up in front of a judge and say those
words, because I feel fortunate to be here in the United States.
I could have ended up anywhere. When The Mom and The Dad
realized they had to leave Egypt before something bad happened

to The Dad, he could have chosen to go to almost any country. He chose the United States, and I have to say that it was probably one of the few good choices that man ever made.

Before I could send my naturalization application in, I had to go to a local Walgreens to have my passport photos taken. I was giddy with excitement as the photographer clicked my image into her camera.

I then had to submit a number of supporting papers, such as copies of my tax records and green card. And I had to go in to be fingerprinted. I had prints on file with my local police department through the Police Explorer Program, but I guess the federal government needed their own set.

To help me with the naturalization process, I found an immigration lawyer through Andrew Kline, one of the lawyers who had helped me with the case against The Mom and The Dad. Andrew referred me to the Seyfarth Shaw legal practice, which specializes in immigration issues. Angelo Paparelli was my lawyer there, but I also worked with another of their attorneys, Elizabeth Wheeler. I knew her as Liz.

All in all, the process was lengthy, and the packet I finally turned in was quite extensive. Then I waited. And waited. I was nervous and bit my fingernails down to stubs. After about a month I learned that I had to appear for an interview and a test. Thank goodness the date was some weeks in the future, as it gave me time to study like crazy.

The United States Citizenship and Immigration Services gave

me a booklet to read and a CD to listen to, and I listened to that CD every day in my car as I drove to and from work. Then, at work, I studied during my breaks. I am glad that my friends and coworkers were behind me all the way. They helped me study by asking me questions from the booklet. There were a hundred questions total. Only ten of them would be asked during my citizenship test, but I did not know which ten would be asked, so I was determined to learn the answers to all one hundred.

The help of my friends was important to me because when it comes to studying, my memory is not good. While someone else might read something once and memorize it right away, I have to go over and over and over it before it sticks. I believe this is another residual effect of my impoverished time in Egypt and my time in slavery. My brain did not have the opportunity to be educated during my early years, when the brain is most ready to learn. My brain instead learned survival tactics, which are important too. But to function best in society today, people need to learn how to study. People need to learn how to learn.

Because studying is hard for me, I was relieved to see that some of the questions on the naturalization test were pretty basic, such as, "Who was our first president?" George Washington. "Where is the capitol of our country located?" Washington, DC. "On what day do we celebrate our independence?" July 4th. But some of the questions were much tougher. I had to know how many senators we had. One hundred. Who was president during the Great Depression? Franklin Roosevelt. What do we call the first ten amendments to the Constitution? The Bill of Rights. If both the president and the vice president can no longer serve, who becomes president? The Speaker of the House.

My friends were amazed that I had to learn all that I did, because they didn't know the answers to many of the questions themselves. If you'd like to have some fun, you can go to the US Citizenship and Immigration Services website and look at the naturalization test to see how many of the questions you know the answers to.

One of the questions, though, I knew the answer to inside and out. I had learned it in a history class, and it had stuck with me. The question was: Name a major cause of the Civil War. Slavery. Slavery was a major cause of the American Civil War. I would never forget that, because through that war an end to legalized slavery happened. The Civil War was what had given the United States government legal grounds to rescue me. No, I was not going to miss getting the correct answer to that question!

Another factor of the test had to do with writing. I had become fluent in spoken English, but written English could still pose a challenge. I was glad to learn that most of the test would be oral.

On the day I had my citizenship interview and test, I got into my car and promptly took the wrong freeway. I was going to meet Liz at a government office in Riverside, California, which wasn't that far away. I had been to Riverside countless times, so it is a testament to how nervous I was that I got lost.

Fortunately, I called Liz several times to tell her where I was, and she helped direct me to the right road and the correct build-ing. Getting lost did nothing to calm my nerves. First, the letter I'd gotten that gave me information about my appointment was clear that I should arrive at least fifteen minutes ahead of time. Not only was that not going to happen, but I was going to be at least fifteen minutes late. That in itself was grounds for the appointment to be canceled.

If the appointment were canceled, I would be devastated. I had hoped and dreamed for years about becoming a US citizen, and now here I was fighting off tears as I frantically drove through downtown Riverside. My stomach was in knots and I had trouble catching my breath. My asthma can be stress induced, and I hoped I would not have a major asthma episode before I arrived.

Liz was my calm in the center of the storm. She kept the immigration people informed of my estimated time of arrival and convinced them to hold my appointment. What a relief that was! When I finally arrived, Liz helped me go through the metal detec-tor and led me to the reception area to check in. I had only a few minutes to calm down before a woman came to lead me back to her office. Liz gave me a confident smile as I left to take the most important test of my life.

The lady was nice, but I was quite intimidated by her. Before I could sit down, I had to stand in front of her, raise my right hand, and agree to tell the truth during the course of the test and inter-view. By the time I sat down, I was shaking.

I'd had to bring the original copies of all my documentation with me, and she went through that first. Then I signed a lot of paperwork before we went through the application I had sent in months earlier. She asked me questions about the information I had put on the application, but I knew from Liz that the woman was also assessing my comprehension of the English language, as well as my ability to speak it. Knowing the language is just one of the requirements for citizenship. My remedial English classes paid off, though. This was a part of the test that I knew I was going to pass.

Then the actual test started. There were three parts. The first was the oral test about United States history and government. Of the ten questions she asked me, I had to get six of them correct. When I got six of them right, she would stop asking questions, even though she had not asked all ten. I was nervous during this and don't remember every detail, but I think I knew every question she asked. I got maybe one of them wrong; she might have asked me seven questions.

Part two was the English reading test. The lady put a sentence in front of me, and I had to read it out loud to her. Piece of cake! The third and final part of the test was writing down a sentence that she spoke to me. This was harder for me, and my hand trembled as I fought to keep my grip on the pen. I wrote slowly and deliberately. I looked at the words on the paper as I resisted my impulse to change them. Then I handed the paper to her.

The lady looked at the paper and wrote something down in her notes. Then she signed another piece of paper before she gave it to me. "Congratulations," she said, "on becoming a citizen of the United States."

It took me a second to process what she was saying. Then I realized that I had passed all of the tests, and I began to cry. My years in bondage had not been for nothing. My bondage had brought me here to this great country, and I was now a citizen, with all of its rights and privileges. I could even vote! Well, I could as soon as I went through my upcoming citizenship ceremony and took my Oath of Allegiance to the United States.

When I walked back to the reception area, back to Liz, I felt a rush of relief. It was over. My hours of study, my months of anxiety that I would not pass, or that the government would find some obscure rule that prevented me from becoming a citizen, were over. I was finally as free as anyone else. I had paid a huge price for my freedom. Now I could make real plans to begin helping others find theirs.

Added to the fact that the door was now open for me to become either a police officer or an ICE agent (or both), to become a United States citizen I'd had to renounce my citizenship to Egypt. I was no longer obligated to have anything to do with that country, and I felt as if the last tie that bound me to it had been cut.

I think Liz was about as happy as I was. The first thing she did was take me to Marshalls, a department store that was close by, to buy a frame for me to put my certificate of citizenship in. I knew that was above and beyond what she was required to do as my lawyer, and I appreciated her kind gesture. But she was not done. We then went to lunch at a nice restaurant.

The choice of restaurants was funny because another location of this same restaurant was where my adoptive family and I had gone after my adoption had been completed. We'd had a wonderful time then, and now Liz and I were having another wonderful time celebrating my citizenship.

Because the restaurant was on my way home, I drove my own car and followed Liz. In my haste to get inside the building to take my test, I had forgotten my phone in my car. When I checked it, I had close to a dozen calls from friends who wanted to know if I had passed the test. I was blessed; I could not have any better friends. Some had even called or texted me more than once because they were eager to hear my news. They were unaware that I had been late for the appointment, and they were dying to learn what had happened.

The first call I made was to Daniel. He was extremely excited for me, and I realized for about the thousandth time what a special man he was. He quickly made plans to get off work early so he could take me out to dinner that evening. My next call was to Amber. Without the kindness and generosity she and her family had shown me, I do not know what would have become of me. I could almost see her through the phone connection jumping up and down with joy.

There were so many more people to call, including Teresa, Karla, and PaNou, that I sent out a group text message. All the message said was, I PASSED!

Two people I did not call were my adoptive mom and dad, but out of the blue that evening Steve called me. By this time our communication was not regular, but we did talk—some.

"What are you doing?" he asked.

When I told him I was celebrating the passing of my citizenship test, he got pretty mad because I had not included him. I had not told him I was taking the test that day, and I had not invited him to commemorate the big event with my friends and me.

I didn't have to think twice about why that was. Even though I give credit to Steve for trying to mend fences and establish good relationships with his kids, and even though I had allowed him to stay with me for several months during and after his divorce from my adoptive mom, I was still pretty mad about the money. He and Patty had spent tens of thousands of dollars of my money without my permission, and even though several years had passed, neither parent had made any attempt to pay me back. I was cordial to him, was even encouraged by his efforts to be a good dad, but I felt my anger was justified.

I took my oath and officially became a citizen of the United States on Thursday, December 15, 2011. On that day I dressed carefully in a black shirt and black dress pants, accented with dangly silver earrings and a silver pendant necklace. My long, dark hair hung loose, and my blue eye shadow matched my purse.

The ceremony was being held at the Quiet Cannon country club in Montebello, California, just east of Los Angeles. Amber and Teresa drove in with me, and Mark met us as soon as we arrived. I gave him a big hug. I was glad he was there. I knew without a doubt that without him I would not have been there on that day.

When I walked into the huge room, I was handed a small American flag, which I treasure to this day. There were roughly nine hundred of us becoming citizens, but the room was filled with many more people than that. Over and above the people being naturalized and their many friends and family members, there were a handful of reporters and news cameras. I am sure there were a number of interesting people becoming citizens that day, but the only person these journalists were interested in was me.

Since The Mom and The Dad had been sentenced back in 2006, I had been in the news many times. Southern California news such as the *Los Angeles Times*, television station KTLA, the *Orange County Register*, the Associated Press, and many others had championed me and used my story to bring awareness of human trafficking to the general public. I had spoken several times in the past to some of the reporters who were there at the ceremony. Besides my days as a slave and the details of my rescue, the reporters had been interested in almost everything I did. From my adoption to my high school graduation to my speaking engagements, it always seemed there was a camera pointed at me or a reporter waiting to speak with me.

Most times I did not mind, because I knew that the more people who knew my story, the better chance another person held in bondage had of being rescued. Today I welcomed the reporters. I was so excited that nothing could break my joyful mood. Nothing.

Eventually the voices and stirring in the room settled down and we sat. Before long a federal judge entered the room. I stood, and there, with nearly nine hundred others, I was sworn in as a naturalized US citizen. Afterward, everyone cheered and my friends swarmed me with affection.

When the cameras descended upon me, I told reporters, "I went through something terrible, but right now I'm in a great place. I can't imagine anything greater than having my own life." And that is true. When you are a slave, your life belongs to someone else. It is an unimaginable existence for most people, and I am glad of that. I hope that soon no one will ever have to feel the overwhelming sense of loss, frustration, exhaustion, hunger, demeaning words, and physical abuse that I did.

The day I went through the citizenship ceremony was the greatest day of my life. To come from such extreme poverty and be sold into slavery had done nothing to give me a sense of belonging. After being shuttled across the ocean and then placed into a series of group and foster homes in several different cities, I had ended up with the feeling that I did not belong anywhere. But now I had a place to call home: the United States of America!

Looking ahead, I believe that someday I will become either a police officer or an Immigration and Customs Enforcement agent, and I hope to spend the rest of my life helping others find their way out of slavery. I've come this far, and I know I will get to the finish line.

CHAPTER SEVENTEEN

When I first came to the United States, few people saw me, or even knew I existed, because I was kept inside the house most of the time. But as time went on, I began taking my captors' twin boys across the street to the park, and then to the pool. Other than the Asian woman who looked at me oddly, I do not believe anyone thought there was anything unusual about me. They should have.

Today there are tens of thousands of people being held against their will right here in the United States. Some are domestic servants, like I was. Many others are forced to work in fields or factories, or even perform illegal or sexual acts. If not for a concerned citizen, I might still be held in bondage. I'm not sure what one citizen saw that made him or her pick up the phone to tell the police about me, but it could have been any number of things. Whatever the reason, I am thankful that he or she decided to take action rather than sit and wonder about me.

On the off chance that you have suspicions about a person that you have seen, here are some specific things to look for, along with information on who to call and what to say. It takes only a single phone call to put the steps into action that could rescue someone like me. Remember, though, that small signs are always part of a bigger picture, so be careful not to assume things, and to share your concerns with a trusted adult.

If the person you suspect is a slave is out and about in public, something to look for is the clothes. If you see someone who is dressed in clothes that do not fit, that are more out of style and much dirtier than the people they are with, that could be an indication that the person is a victim of human trafficking.

When I lived with my captors, my clothes were always hand-me-downs. Often my clothes did not fit, and because I was forbidden to use the washing machine, my clothes were never as clean as they should have been. But the factor of clothing by itself is not nearly enough evidence, as there are many people to whom clothing is not important, or who do not have the money to buy nicer things. I have even seen wealthy people shopping in their pajamas in the store where I work, so clothing is only one possible piece to a big puzzle.

Another indication that the person might be held in bondage is the person's level of activity as compared to the people they are with. If the person is dressed poorly and also does not participate in activities along with the people around them, then that could be another red flag. This is especially true if the person you suspect is being held against her will acts in a manner that is subservient to others.

Even though I went to Big Bear Lake, Disneyland, and Sea-World with my captor family, I was not allowed to participate in the fun activities as their children did. I could not go on the rides or swim with the dolphins. And when food or souvenirs were purchased, they were never for me.

I was never taken to a store, but if I had been, I might have carried packages while my captors carried nothing. I would have walked behind The Mom or The Dad and kept my eyes lowered. Outside, in a place like a park, a person in bondage might give water to captors who are playing football. The slave would gather everyone's belongings and carry them to the car while everyone else socialized at a picnic.

If you see a poorly dressed person who seems to be in a servant's position, another big indicator is his or her demeanor. A person held in bondage will have a completely different manner about them than someone who is gainfully employed. A slave will keep his eyes downcast, even when he speaks to others. This is a different kind of downcast than someone who is shy. There will probably be sadness in his facial expression and an aura of defeat in the way he carries himself. This person will walk and move in a manner that is deferential to the people around him. And he will keep himself some distance away, usually coming toward others only when asked to do so.

If I ever saw a person who acted frightened or cowed, especially around certain people, I know I would pay special attention, because that's exactly how I behaved when I was with The Mom and The Dad, or any of their family members. I was terrified that I would do, or not do, something and that my action or lack of it would get me slapped.

Being called "stupid girl" for many years damaged my self-esteem. Words can be hurtful, and if you hear hurtful words directed at you over a long period of time, something inside you begins to believe them. Because of that, the way I walked and moved indicated my total submission to the members of my captor family.

How the person speaks is another sign. Most people enslaved here in the United States have been brought here illegally from other countries. The slave might not understand English, so the people around her speak to her in another language. If you approached her to ask a question, she might give you a frightened or confused look, then someone else, maybe a captor, would answer on her behalf. He might tell you she is deaf, autistic, nonverbal, or visiting from another country—any story to deflect your interest and suspicion.

I learned early on that I was never to speak unless I was spoken to first, and then I was only to answer the question, or indicate that I understood the instruction. Any other communication could earn me a slap, and chitchat was out of the question.

The group of people the person is with is another indicator that something might be wrong. Do others speak to the person in a rude and demanding manner? Do they never include the person in conversation? Do these people act in a way that seems entitled? Do they act superior to everyone else? If so, these people might be like The Mom and The Dad. They could be captors, and guilty of illegal human trafficking or holding someone against their will.

Never have I met another person who behaved in such an entitled way as The Mom did. Nothing was ever good enough for her, and she made that clear to whoever was in the house, even when friends of the family came to stay. Captors often feel they deserve better than anyone else, and that attitude shows in everything they do.

Keeping odd hours is another indicator. I believe the person who called about me had seen me repeatedly late at night washing dishes. If you see a child at a time when you shouldn't, or in a place where a child should not be, or doing an activity a child should not be doing, that should be a red flag. The same goes for adults. Odd activity, odd hours should be noted.

The final major sign is the person's speech. Not the language they speak—although, not knowing English or not speaking it can be an indicator—but how they speak is important. If the person you think is being held in bondage does not look at you when you or others speak to him, if he mumbles or seems fearful when spoken to, that could be an indicator that something is wrong.

On the day I was rescued, I knew three words in English: "hi," "dolphin," and "stepsister." I now believe my captors intentionally kept anything from me that might teach me the language, because knowledge of English could have given me some power. Something captors do well is keep their slaves powerless.

It is important to know that none of these factors, either individually or together, necessarily mean that a person is being held against their will. I am sure there are many people who have all of these factors who are not toiling away in slavery. But they could be. It is possible that they could be, and it's that fact that is critical. If you think someone is being held, you then have to decide what to do. Will you do the right thing, or the wrong? If you do nothing and the person is in need of help, that would be a tragedy. You might be that person's only hope. You might be the only person who notices that something is off. You could be the person who changes someone else's life for the better.

On the other hand, if you say something and the person turns out to be happy, healthy, and interacting of their own free will with the people they live and work with, then all that has been lost is some of your time and the time of a few people from your local police or social services department. Even though many of the people at these departments are overworked and the departments are often understaffed, my experience has been that helping a person out of bondage is something they absolutely want to do.

If you are not sure if someone is being held, a private discussion with people you trust is always a good idea. If you have surrounded yourself with good people, then they will most likely give you good advice. If not, find someone you trust: a teacher, counselor, pastor, or family friend.

If you decide that action is in order, the first step is to call the non-emergency line for your local police department. Then give the dispatcher a brief rundown of the situation. You could say, for example, "I think my neighbors are involved in human trafficking and slavery, because I regularly see a child working in the house late at night. This child never goes to school, and on the rare times when I have seen her in the yard, she acts as if she does not speak or understand English."

Those words are probably similar to the words that were used to bring attention to my captors and to me. It's only a few sentences, and you can remain anonymous if you want.

What happens next will probably depend on what state you live in and the specific circumstances about the people in question. Is the suspected slave a child or an adult? What is the person being held in bondage being forced to do? What are their living conditions? Do they speak English? Are they United States citizens? The answers to these questions, along with many more, will determine the next course of action.

More than likely some member of law enforcement will interview you either by phone or in person. Your information will then be included in their investigation. It may take many weeks, but when officials are sure, they will plan a rescue, and possibly an arrest. You, however, may never know the details, or the result.

When I was rescued, I had no idea that people who worked for the United States government had been planning for weeks to rescue me. What I knew at the time was that people came into the house, and one of them pulled me out. I did not know that many carefully detailed plans had been made, along with contingencies. If The Dad did or said this, then officials would move here and do that. If The Mom was home, then people would move to this specific location inside the house. My rescuers planned for every possibility to make my rescue as safe as it could be for me.

I was beyond terrified when I was rescued. For years I had been told that if the police came to get me, bad things would happen, things that were far worse than what I'd lived with every day. Plus, bad things would happen to my family back in Egypt. That's why I was mistrustful and afraid to admit anything to my rescuers about my circumstances. Ten years later I am still slow to trust, and may always be. Many rescued slaves are like this. They don't know whom to trust and, like me at that point in time, may know nothing about the customs or legal system in the United States.

Living in bondage might be all the person can remember. He or she might be frightened to be out of captivity and not know which end is up. They need time. It was only around those few people who gently, constantly, and consistently asked if I was okay, if I needed anything, that I let my guard down.

Mark Abend was one of these people. He acted like he cared, and over time I realized that he truly did. But a former slave won't come to that conclusion quickly. She won't be pressured. She won't operate on your time frame. She might not even be cooperative—at first. If she is lucky enough to have quality people around her as I did, then she will come around. Eventually.

After I was rescued and had time to think, I made a decision. I knew I could do one of two things. I could become a helpful resource to my rescuers and move on with my life, or draw into myself and become a victim. I wanted a full life. I wanted to live, to leave my past in the past, so for me there was only one choice. God was part of my decision too. I felt in my heart that He had worked hard to get me rescued, so I needed to honor His work by making as much out of my life as I could. And I have.

More than seventeen thousand new slaves are brought into the United States every year. And more are being rescued than ever before. That's why it is important to know that a rescued slave could show up in your school, workplace, or neighborhood. That person is going to need a lot of love, care, and patience.

If your path crosses that of a former slave in a legal, professional, or friendship capacity, I hope you understand that they may not want to talk about it. Instead of pushing, be tolerant. Be kind and caring. Most of all, be a friend, because you may be the only friend this newly rescued person has.

I am lucky to have found wonderful friends who have become my surrogate family. These people are small in number but huge in heart, and I trust them completely. That is something I could not have done a few short years ago. I look at my life now and see only a future where I will do even more to stop human trafficking.

If this book leads to even a single rescue, then my time in bondage was worth it.

I believe there is a reason, a purpose, for everything in this life, and I know that my purpose is to help put a permanent stop to this terrible crime. With the help of your vigilant eyes and ears, every child, every person, can live a wonderful life of their own choosing. I not only believe this *can* happen. I believe it will.

EPILOGUE

The day before I took my citizenship test, I realized I was pregnant. Talk about a nerve-wracking day! I was already nervous about taking the test. Much rested on my becoming a citizen. One way or another I was going into law enforcement to help catch other human traffickers and also help people like me who have been held in bondage. But first I had to become a citizen of the United States.

If the test weren't enough stress, realizing that I was pregnant put my emotions completely over the top. My relationship with Daniel had become quite serious, but like many young people, we had not planned a pregnancy. I was concerned about what his reaction to the news might be and I was anxious about how the pregnancy would affect my rheumatoid arthritis.

Amber was the first person I called. She came over and we got five different pregnancy tests—to be absolutely sure. All were positive. Now that I knew for sure that a baby was on the way, Amber helped me focus on the most immediate issue, passing my citizenship test. I would still be pregnant after the test, and could deal with my feelings about it at that time. We spent the rest of the evening studying.

The next day I realized that Amber was right. After I passed my test, I took time to make more sense of what was going on inside my body. At this time Daniel and I had been dating for about nine months. We were still trying to sort out what our future was long term. How would the baby affect that? I wondered.

My pregnancy is proof that the only surefire method of birth control is abstinence, so I hope young men and women who read this book consider that before they let hormones and young love take over. A baby is an expensive responsibility—one that changes your life, usurps your time, and keeps you from fun times with your friends. But I knew right away that I was up for it. I wanted to keep my baby.

Part of my decision was based on the fact that I did not want to do to my son or daughter what my parents had done to me. I could not imagine anyone else raising my child, and I knew from that point on that even though I was going to have a career in law enforcement, my life was now dedicated to the best interests of my child.

I was quite nervous regarding my potential parenting skills because I didn't have too many positive mom role models to draw from. But Amber, Teresa, Karla, PaNou, and my other friends made me understand that what I needed to do was act out of love. Love was what drove a mother's instinct and was what would carry a family through. That, along with a few parenting books!

I didn't tell Daniel for several weeks because it took that long for me to process this little surprise. I also went to the doctor before I told him. That way I would have all the facts I needed to pass along to him. When I finally broke the news, Daniel went through the same gamut of emotions that I had, including shock, nervousness, and fear.

On top of starting to integrate the idea of a baby into our lives, we had to figure out what to do about us. We decided that when my lease ran out on my apartment, I would move in with him. Daniel had recently bought a three bedroom home. He didn't have any furniture yet, so when we moved mine in, the house looked great.

By the time I was four months along, we had both adjusted to the idea of coparenting our baby. Daniel's large family was supportive, as were my friends. I began to feel much calmer about my ability to parent a child and about the future of Daniel and me as a couple. By my fourth-month appointment Daniel and I were beyond thrilled to see the shape of our little girl on the ultrasound. We stared and stared at the image on the monitor. This was our baby!

People have told me what wise choices I have made in my friends, and my friends do encourage me a lot. Anything I need, no matter what it is, they are there to help. Daniel is the same way. He is truly one in a million and started becoming an active dad well before Athena was born. He read many books on pregnancy and babies, and about becoming a dad. He went to every doctor's appointment with me and was kind and caring on days when I was not feeling well.

Many women with rheumatoid arthritis find that their symptoms lessen when they are expecting, and that was true for me. Most of my symptoms were still there, but not to the same extent as before I was pregnant and after our baby arrived. I didn't want to do anything that might harm Athena before she was born, so I stopped taking all of my RA medication. I had a single steroid shot during my pregnancy, because the pain and stiffness had gotten bad enough that I couldn't stand it, but other than that, until I stopped breast-feeding, my medication consisted of hot baths and walking.

Athena was due on July 23, 2012, but I was scheduled to be induced on July 19 because Athena was becoming too heavy for my arthritic legs to handle. Daniel and I decided in the beginning that we wanted to raise our daughter to be a strong woman who felt free to express her own thoughts and ideas. We didn't have to worry about that, because Athena was already taking charge. On the way to the hospital to be induced, my water broke. Our baby was going to be born on her terms.

Several hours later I held our six pound, fifteen-ounce bundle of joy. The look of pure love on Daniel's face was indescribable, and I was so overcome with emotion that I could barely breathe. We had been excited to see what our baby would look like, and I was thrilled to see Daniel's cheeks and my nose. Athena is the perfect combination of us both.

My early misgivings aside, I have found that I love being a mom. If I have a fault here, it is that I snuggle with Athena too much. I never want to put her down. I am totally attached to her, but she is attached to her daddy, too. Daniel has turned out to be such a great dad. He changes more than his share of diapers and loves caring for her as much as I do. Daniel and I want the best for Athena, so we have begun putting money away for her college education.

Because of Athena, my priorities in life have both changed and become more solid. Everything I do in life now will be to make her feel safe, secure, and happy. But because of Athena I want to become a police officer or ICE agent more than ever. I want to show my daughter that women can make a difference in areas where change is most needed. I want to impress upon her that in addition to making a wonderful home she can be an active, productive, successful woman outside of the house. The best way I can show her how to do that is to lead by example. Plus, the last thing I want Athena to be is the cowed, subservient, naïve, uneducated young girl that I was. Athena may have put my law enforcement goals on hold for a year or so, but I *will* get there.

I want Athena to have the sense of family that I missed out on. She has a wonderful set of grandparents on her dad's side, as well as many loving aunts, uncles, and cousins. While there is no biological family in my life right now, my friends Amber, Teresa,

PaNou, Karla, and many others have become my family here in the United States. My definition of "family" is those people who will love and support you no matter what, and these people do that for me.

I don't know why my early life was as hard and unfair as it was, but our experiences—good and bad—shape us into who we become. Today I am completely happy and look forward to many wonderful years with my family and friends. I also look forward to putting a few captors behind bars. If you are a trafficker, watch out. I am getting ready to come after you. I know that eventually we will put an end to the terrible custom of slavery. I hope that it is sooner rather than later. With everyone's help and support, maybe my wish will come true.

Mahshi Warak Areesh Recipe

1 lb. fresh tender grape leaves

1½ cups uncooked rice

2 cups ground or chopped meat, preferably lamb

1 medium-size tomato, chopped (optional)

1½ tsp. salt

½ tsp. pepper

½ tsp. cinnamon

2 cups cold water

2 medium-size tomatoes, sliced

2 whole garlic bulbs (a bulb is the whole head of garlic)

Several meat bones

8 garlic cloves crushed with salt

½ cup lemon juice

1 tsp. dried mint

Soften and blanch grape leaves by dipping a few at a time in boiling, salted water. Set aside.

Wash rice, and mix with ground meat, chopped tomato, salt, pepper, cinnamon, and ½ cup cold water.

Stuff one leaf at a time: Place a teaspoon of stuffing in the center of the leaf. Then fold the bottom of the leaf up over the stuffing, fold from each side to the middle, and roll tightly to form a cylinder about three inches long and somewhat thicker than a cigar.

Place layer of tomato slices with whole garlic, meat bones, and crushed garlic with salt in bottom of pressure cooker pan.

Cover with the stuffed leaves arranged side by side in layers.

Sprinkle with lemon juice and add salt to taste.

Add remaining water. Cook under pressure for 12 minutes.

Open cooker and simmer uncovered until sauce is thickened.

Taste sauce. Add more lemon and salt if necessary, then allow leaves to cool in sauce.

Drain sauce into a bowl.

Lift rolls out one by one and arrange on serving platter. Cover with sauce. Serve cold. Prepare a day ahead, if possible, for best flavor.